To L
Your Kindness
Makes Everyones Day,
"X 2007"

Philosophy of "X"
Revealing the True Meaning of Life
By "X"

To Lynn,
Your Kind Attitude
Makes Everyones Day,
"Jason"

The Philosophy of "X" – Copyright ©2007 "X"

Printed and bound in the United States of America. All rights reserved. No part of this book may be reproduced in any form or by any electronic or mechanical means including information storage and retrieval systems without permission in writing from the author or publisher, except by a reviewer, who may quote brief passages in a review. First edition.

Library of Congress Cataloging in Publication Data

Philosophy - Science of Humanity

Philosophy - Past, present, and future

Health - exercise, mental, physical, spiritual

Book Cover – by David Bey www.designismylife.com

Editor – Rhonda Powell - United Publishing Press

Co-Editor – Jomo Yakini - ATL, GA

Table of Contents

PROLOGUE	7
INTRODUCTION	8
GOD	12
LIFE	14
THE GAME	17
ENERGY AND MATTER	20
LIFE'S GREAT ILLUSIONS	22
PEACE	24
AWARENESS	26
PERSONALITY [MASTER KEY CHAPTER]	31
EMOTIONS [MASTER KEY CHAPTER]	41
SURVIVAL	50
DEATH	53
FEAR [MASTER KEY CHAPTER]	55
RELATIONSHIPS [MASTER KEY CHAPTER]	59
LOVE	64
THE HISTORY OF ROMANCE	71
SEX	73
TRUTH	77
COMMUNICATION	81
HEALTH [MASTER KEY CHAPTER]	85
INTEGRITY	100
TIME	103
PROBLEMS	105
SOCIETY	108
GOOD AND BAD	110
GENIUS	113

DRUGS	115
RELIGION	118
EDUCATION	121
POLITICS	123
MONEY [MASTER KEY CHAPTER]	126
RACE	133
POWER	136
INVENTION	139
WAR	142
CHILDREN	145
MUSIC	151
APPEARANCE	154
IN CONCLUSION [MASTER KEY CHAPTER]	157

Master Key Chapters contain practical exercises necessary for peaceful and happy life development.

PROLOGUE

For most of my life I pondered and prayed for the wisdom to be a better man and to understand why life is so friggin' hard. Why did I have to live through so many of life's unpredictable hardships and troubling circumstances? At the age of 19, I seriously began therefore, to study the functional physical world of the universe. I spent countless hours of study including ancient and modern mental technologies, eastern and western philosophies, theology, world history, nutrition, anthropology, politics, psychology, biology, economics, personal life experiences, and deep protracted meditative introspection.

It was tedious work with many hardships and great moments of joy. As I became more learned in the governing situations of life, I eventually came to this realization. All the knowledge in the world means nothing to my wellbeing if it is not available to the world. This is an average man's attempt to share with the world his love of Humanity by doing my part to create a vested interest in others of the greater virtues of philosophy. To love, to honor, and to respect the Creator in all it's resplendent glory by learning what it truly means to be Human.

Welcome to my world, your world, our world within the pages of this book – *Philosophy of "X"* – written by the author simply known as "X". Enjoy.

INTRODUCTION

First of all, let it be perfectly understood that nothing pertinent to being Human should be a mystery. Other than the unforeseeable day-to-day occurrences, everything has a clear and decisive explanation. As children we have a natural, healthy curiosity about life and everything in it. Eventually as we grow, we begin to grasp a clear understanding of speech and the ability to use it to find out the answers to things, but oftentimes our older siblings, friends, and controlling adults inadvertently stunt our natural childlike inquisitiveness.

Children may ask questions like the following:

Why am I here? What is God? Is there a reason for life? Why is life so hard?

Questions like these are often dismissed as silly, totally unimportant, or the makings of fantastical delusions of grandeur. The question is "Why do we as adults have no answers to these questions?" Adults smother these questions away so that they will not look stupid to anyone – especially their children. Adults even hide away questions about life from themselves answering a child's questions from this seemingly safe point of view.

Adults may answer children's questions like so:

Stop asking those silly questions.

I don't know the answer to the question so stop asking.

One of my favorites is "I really don't know the truth," or the answer, "I will make up a make-believe answer." It's not the truth but the child will like it, and I will be the smart one looking great in this situation. Thus the fairy tale was born giving birth to the beloved city of Hollywood that makes billions of dollars yearly in the process of make-believe fulfillment. Don't you just love it?

INTRODUCTION

Ladies and Gentlemen:

Cover it up all you want. The legitimate questions you had about life as a child are still there and still waiting to be answered. Just be open to the information and be prepared to enjoy life with renewed confidence and awareness. I strongly suggest that you read the chapters in the order they are presented or you will be lost because you may not see the relation of one subject to the next. It will be like watching a movie in the middle, first you will get some but not the full understanding of the subject matter. Fight the temptation to jet to the sex, drugs, and relationships sections. Please follow the prescribed protocol when reading this book so you can acquire the knowledge that you paid for.

Unfortunately, many educational institutions, public organizations, social programs, and schools of every order claim to know, or suggest that they know all the truth that you need to live a carefree successful Life. Let me tell you family and friends, no one book, no dogma, no philosophy is the "know it all - tell all" when it comes to the answers of life. If that were the case, why go to school to learn a trade, the sciences, or anything for that matter. Not even this book is all that because transition, (or change if you like) is an ongoing ever changing process. I wish I could make this outlandish claim with my edifying book Brothers and Sisters, but that would be the biggest hypocritical lie of all.

Institutions, organizations, programs, and schools do in fact provide you with truth because truth is universal. However, they usually only provide you with bits and pieces of the truth enough to keep you blinded from the whole truth, to keep you around for a while and distracted from the whole truth. Willfully or unknowingly, I leave that up to your bright minds to decide.

In Philosophy of "X", I provide eye-opening keys to the truths of the universe. Straight forward and head on!

So this is the format you need to undertake to understand the following information:
1. Keep an open mind.
2. Don't be so serious while reading and participating with this book. Have fun with it. After all you paid for it, so be entertained.
3. That's it, simple.

My fellow philosophers I could have written this book very formally like many other books of philosophy. So much so that you might think that you need to be sitting in a very big chair with a fancy tobacco pipe in your mouth with me putting on a stuffy façade that I am some kind of all-powerful guru of some sort. That's just not my style people. I put my pants on one leg at a time just like you do. To "X" a day without laughter is like a day without breathing. Learning can be great fun so let's have some fun.

> It is easier to live through someone else than to become complete yourself.
> – Betty Friedan

I strongly implore you to embark on a journey with me to finally see what life is all about and in the process, accomplish the greatest understanding of all, the understanding of yourself unedited, unflinching, and uncut.

Now that I have stated that everything has a clear explanation, take everything that you read from here on out in this book as being 100% absolutely and irrefutably – a LIE. "Yes Ma'am" and "Yes, Sir" – a LIE, a brilliant, boisterous, brazen, cornucopia of insightful hogwash. You have nothing to fear but fear itself. Read on if you dare. I double dog dare you to go where few have ever gone before. I must insist that you enjoy reading these pitiful entertaining lies. What is life without the joy? It's a big steaming pile of poop without joy. So enjoy the book. Learn something if you must, and I humbly thank you for your time and contribution.

> If you make people think they're thinking, they'll love you: but if you really make them think, they'll hate you.
> – *Don Marquis*

> I know you're out there. I can feel you now. I know that you're afraid. You're afraid of us. You're afraid of change. I don't know the future. I didn't come here to tell you how this is going to end. I came here to tell you how it's going to begin. I'm going to hang up this phone, and then I'm going to show these people what you don't want them to see. I'm going to show them a world... without you. A world without rules and controls. Without borders or boundaries. A world where anything is possible. Where we go from there, is a choice I leave to you.
> – *Neo - Movie - The Matrix*

> The great masses of people more easily fall victim to a big lie than to a small one.
> – *Adolf Hitler*

GOD

"What is God?"

Simply put, God is energy of unfathomable abundance, with a constant ongoing awareness of itself, a being of great significance encompassing unlimited boundaries. After all it is the creator of all things.

Another way to view God is to say that God is the Supreme Thinker. Greater than anything we could ever create even with the most advanced computers on turbo boosters cannot touch it.

For those who do not believe in God, or a Supreme Being, let me offer an example – a case in point.

Case in Point:

Without the pollination of plants here on Earth by insects the "world" as we know it would cease to exist.

No pollination = no plants.

No plants = no food or oxygen

Hence, no life present at all, except the possibility of single-celled creatures, fish, and a few cockroaches here and there – but no people.

You could possibly assume that an insect with no brain can figure out that the pollen it collects from plant to plant sustains nearly all life on the planet, even itself?? Or that plants (also without a brain), realize that its life and the rest of Life on earth depend on it attracting enough brainless insects to provide for its own reproduction?? Or is it simply an outside intelligence calling the shots to ensure that the balance of life goes on? Assuming you have a functional brain of course, you be the judge.

People in their infinite wisdom sometimes speculate that God is a male/father, female/mother, or none of the above. For the sake of argument, let's check into a few things:

Scientifically on planet Earth the only reasons that two sexes exist within this physical plane are for reproduction and pleasure. Scientist also speculate that if a species were to be created for the first time that the first of its kind would have to be a female because a male cannot possibly have a baby. It simply does not make sense to create a male first. The creator would have to at least make both sexes at the same exact time, which is highly improbable. Making things appear out of sequence in an ordered physical plane would wreak havoc with the laws of physics not to mention common sense.

So if all things come from God and if God has a female or male sex "Is it for the same reasons we have sexes on Earth for reproduction and pleasure if we were created in its own image?" Are there a Mister and Misses God? Does God need a physical body to carouse around in? Why does an all-powerful being need a separate sexual identity? Could the image of God we are created in simply be the energy that animates these bodies made up of inanimate elements brought to life? You be the judge. Personally I prefer the energy logic.

> We turn to God for help when our foundations are shaking, only to learn that it is God who is shaking them.
> – Charles C. West

Sometimes people ask, "If God created us then who created God?" This question is of course asinine since it cannot possibly be answered. People just love the drama sometimes, even if it is a waste of time with unanswerable questions.

To sum it up God is a wonderfully all-powerful being with limitless intelligence, sexless, and eternal.

LIFE

"What is Life?" "Why am I here?"

You may or may not believe in God that is your right. So the following explanation may or may not suffice. But please do not let this detour you from reading the book because if nothing else, this is an entertaining string of lies!

God is not unlike other sentient (smart) life forms. It became self-aware only to a much greater extent because by the way, it is God.

Just imagine waking up one day and realizing that you are God. *You* are the most powerful being in all of existence, but in the next instant *you* also realize, "Hey! I'm all alone here. There is just me, and I sure am bored. I could use some company." Imagine a youthful being with the power to create at will. It would be like a child having free reign in a candy store. Enter the creation of the cosmos. The brilliant lights and sounds of countless stars, moons, comets, asteroids, and such are meager playthings to the might of this being. After so many trillions of years even the brilliance of the cosmos can lose some of its luster. Celestial cosmic bodies as great as they are cannot think, feel, and play games with one another. So playtime for God became the very creation of life itself. Creations of countless living creatures' ensued. Abundant plants, insects, and animals flourish on the Earth. Once again God becomes bored and decides it needs some creatures with a little more kick. Enter two legged mammalian hominids known as Human Beings.

"What is the *meaning* of Life?"

God created every thing for one reason and one reason only...

To know what life is like – outside of itself. Other living things provide the experience of life for *God*. It's the ultimate symbiotic relationship. (Symbiotic means, when one or more different species depend on each others help for survival, or just to make their lives more comfortable or interesting).

One of my personal favorite symbiotic relationships is the Human and Friendly Flora (nice bacteria) relationship. When Humans eat stuff most of it is digested inside the intestines where billions of living Friendly Flora call home sweet home. The Friendly Flora eats the stuff we eat and in the process helps us to digest the food, so that we both can live. It's a conveniently neat relationship. The Friendly Flora must also like music because they are largely responsible for the flatulence our bodies produce. (Flatulence is the somewhat malodorous bio-gas known as burps and farts.) Sweet music to the friendly Floras' ears, if they had ears. See if you can find other symbiotic relationships in nature or in general.

So God can feel, see, hear, taste, touch, and experience everything that *everything* does and that in my opinion is better than any movie or Broadway play can ever be. I only wish I could buy a ticket to that show. What a trip! Still need more on the meaning of Life? Read on to the next Chapter.

For the sake of argument: many people have heated discussions about the Darwin Theory that states that modern man evolved from apes. I will answer this question for you once and for all.

If you believe that man evolved from apes you are 100% right.

If you believe that man did not evolve from the apes you are 100% right. Why? It's a theory that means it can't be proven wrong or right beyond a scientific shadow of doubt. Unless one of you geniuses invents a workable time machine that can take you to the very dawn of mans creation and see it with your own eyes, take pictures and videos, and broadcast it on the television for the world to see, this question can't possibly be answered in a scientifically sound manner. Life is short so don't waste too much of your precious lifespan on communication that does not promote peace and harmony in your world.

Knowledge itself is power.
— *Sir Francis Bacon*

Truth, medical research, fun — the holy trinity of the thinking person.
— *Penn Jillette of Penn and Teller -TV Show - Bulls#*!*

Rules for Being Human:

- You will learn lessons.

- There are no mistakes — only lessons.

- A lesson is repeated until it is learned.

- If you don't learn easy lessons, they get harder.
  (Pain is one way the universe gets your attention.)

- You'll know when you've learned a lesson when your actions change.
  — *Unknown*

THE GAME

> You can have it all. You just can't have it all at once.
> – Oprah Winfrey

Let's all play a football game. Let's take away all of the rules and tell all the tremendously buff athletic players that they have all won the game without lifting a finger. Yeah baby! Yeah! Wooooo! Then I welcome you to Dullsville, USA.

Now lets' start over and play the game differently. Add some rules, scores, controlled violence, different attitudes, and create that one of the opposing sides is the winner, and one is the loser. Lets not forget the thousands of fans at the game and the millions of fans watching the game on the boob tube (television) lying about what they would do to win the game if they were actually there in the football game. Now that is a game worth playing – interesting to participate in and to watch. Bingo! Billions of dollars in earnings created yearly and bragging rights for the teammates and fans until next time. Now the game is really super-duper fun!

"What is The Game?"

Everything that is or ever will be is a part of a very elaborate calculated Game. The Game was invented by God (the Supreme Being) to give Life meaning. No game in existence would make Life unbearably dull and pointless, a space of complete and utter boredom.

We are all part of the Grandest Game of all because unlike other earth-bound beings, humans do not have a locked in set of boundaries to stop them from creating games and we can change the game endlessly to our whims' delight.

Case in Point:

A cow cannot leave the fields, put on fancy designer clothing, and go to a gourmet restaurant for a prepared meal by a famous loud mouthed chef (at least not without a little help), but humans can. We are therefore the greatest game pieces on earth and you thought chess pieces were fantastic. So life, just like any other Game, has to have basic rules with foreseeable possible results such as whom or what will win or lose. That's right people – fierce and ugly competition.

In life, "winning" and "losing" is what we, as human beings tend to focus on. In doing so, we lose the true focus on the one absolute goal of the Game of Life.

And that goal is PEACE.

Every thing that you do or any creature ever does in existence is to achieve Peace. From the tiniest one celled organism to the burliest of lumberjacks Peace is where it's at – even if the peace achieved is just for a single brief moment in time. Peace is the greatest satisfaction of all, beyond winning or losing at the game of Life.

So Peace is established as the ultimate goal, or purpose, of all Life. Humans, because of our reasoning capabilities, try to attain peace in many ways; some play sports/games, some pursue money, some use drugs, some eat lots of comfort food, some help other people or living things (or both). Some become rulers of countries and kill millions of other humans in the process all for the hope of achieving Peace.

> If you kill one person it's a tragedy, if you kill a million it's only a statistic.
> – *Josef Stalin - Late Ruler of the former U.S.S.R. - Responsible for the Deaths of 20 Million of his own Russian People - There are Less than 10 Million People in the Entire State of Georgia in the U.S.A.*

THE GAME

Human beings do all of these things, and more, to attain a sense of inner peace. "If I am rich enough, powerful enough, smart enough, calm enough, pretty enough, good enough, sexy enough, take no crap from anyone enough, etc… I will achieve peace." These are some thoughts that rule our lives by the different ways we search for peace and these thoughts and pursuits ultimately leave us empty – and dissatisfied. In this way, it is clear that peace is the goal of Life and we tend to forget the one thing that we really want is P-E-A-C-E.

The Game, therefore, is Life. The Goal of Life is Peace. The central rule of the Game of Life is that as human beings, we make the rules of the game.

True, you are influenced by all the other rule-makers in life: i.e. schools, governments, religious organizations, peers, parents, communities, etc., but *you* choose to accept their rules and make them your own. You choose in order that you may find peace within yourself.

Boys and Girls, Ladies and Gentlemen: *YOU* make the rules by which you live your life so keep your rules simple and straight, and Peace will be close at hand. Rarely, if ever, is Peace a constant reality, but that is the nature of The Game always in transition.

> Do or do not… there is no try.
> – Yoda -Wise Leader of the Jedi Council - Movie - Star Wars

ENERGY AND MATTER

Say for instance, that I put you inside a completely barren room, unclothed, accessory and jewelry-free, completely naked inside an equally naked blank room (nothingness). Now I give you the power to create, but you can use nothing other than what is there in the room.

Now create. I'm waiting. What?? You have nothing to use to create? Sure you do. You have yourself / your body. In just this way, the Creator used its body to create all things. Of course, the Creators "body" is not like our body. Thus, all energy/matter is part of the Creator, formed or transformed for different uses but from the same source nonetheless. Therefore, all energy / matter is the same, so much, in effect, that energy/matter moves in and of itself.

To simplify this statement more, everything is God from the dirt in the carpet, to the clouds in the sky. It all just circulates throughout the universes transitioning to other planes of existence as God sees fit, but never separate because it is the very substance of God.

Human beings are all linked to every part of matter and energy, even that which appears to be separated by time and space, even if it's light years away.

"What is energy / matter?"

Energy and Matter, as far as is discernable, is the electric and elemental stuff that makes up every thing in the known world that is any thing. Most people can agree that there was nothing before there was something, and that "something" is named as God (Creator / Source). It is scientifically proven beyond doubt that matter and energy cannot be destroyed, just transformed to other states of existence.

ENERGY AND MATTER

Energy/matter cannot be destroyed because if that were possible, the Creator itself could be harmed, since the creator is the source and substance of all things. Even your favorite meal, snack, or soft drink is God transitioning from one shape to the next. Have you eaten your helping of the creator today? Now you're given even more reason to bless the food before you dig in to sate your appetite.

LIFE'S GREAT ILLUSIONS

> Between 1450 and 1750 more than 100,000 people, most of them women, were prosecuted by secular and ecclesiastical courts in different parts of Europe for allegedly practicing harmful magic and worshipping the devil. Why did these trials take place? Why did they suddenly proliferate at this particular time in European history? Why were more witches prosecuted in some countries than others? Who were the accused and who were their accusers? And why, after more than 200 years, did the trials eventually draw to an end?
> – *Brian Levack - Author - The Witch Hunt in Early Modern Europe*

> What luck for rulers that men do not think.
> – *Adolf Hitler*

There are many Great Illusions in life, all of which you may or may not be familiar with. Always seek out the truth of things with whatever educational, scientific, mathematical, self-reasoning, life experience, historical, and anthropological data you have at your disposal. Because everything transforms, everything has potential meaning, and everything has other unforeseen reasons for being - in all probability.

It is in fact arguable that life itself is an illusion. Mind-boggling as it may seem if you can understand that all energy / matter comes from and exists in a constant, all-encompassing state. As human beings we can transform ourselves directly and indirectly in non-concrete ways that in itself indicates that life is an illusionary state of being. In other words to create something reality has to be as pliable as molding clay and the thoughts and actions of the molder will determine the outcome of how the molded object will exist in the world.

LIFE'S GREAT ILLUSIONS

How can you ever create something that never existed if this were not the case?

Also, the creator retains ownership of all things so that we humans cannot truly own anything, no matter what. We only have the privilege of sharing things with each other or hogging things for ourselves as long as we can. Do you know the same water that we drink the *DINOSAURS* drank (it's forever recycled). Even our physical bodies are rentals one day to return to raw elements. If we cannot own anything permanently, it can be an illusion. Everything is "nothing," and nothing is everything, so play the game of life as if you have nothing to lose because in fact, that is the truth.

It is preferable to do this in your body in a positive way so you can stick around for a while of course. Illusion or not, life is upon us and things are as they are. Look more closely at the illusions of life and point out your illusions. Don't be scared. None of it is real anyway. Remember, all of the contents of this book are to be considered a lie.

> The important thing in life is not to stop questioning.
> – Albert Einstein

> Believe nothing just because a so-called wise person said it. Believe nothing just because a belief is generally held. Believe nothing just because it is said in ancient books. Believe nothing because it is said to be of divine origin. Believe nothing just because someone else believes it. Believe only what you yourself test and judge to be true.
> – Buddha

> We live in a world of many illusions and much of human belief and behavior is ritualized nonsense.
> – Wes "Scoop" Nisker

PEACE

"What is Peace?"

Peace is the goal of all Life. Why is Peace the goal of all Life? Because peace is a common goal that we can all respect, love, and put in place in our daily lives. Peace is the calm in the eye of the storm, the smile of an innocent child, the love of a best friend. Peace is Joy and joy is peace. The definition really lacks the proper eloquence in our human understanding.

For the sake of argument: Some people think that the pursuit of happiness and obtaining happiness is the goal of life. Let's say you're absolutely right about happiness being the goal of life. I love being happy. It's all the rage on planet Earth. Now if you would please answer these questions for me. How long will your happiness last if you are not at peace? Will it even be possible to be happy without peace in the first place? Case closed – peace wins!

Playing the Game of Life and lessening our responsibilities by not making an effort to properly edify/teach/share life transforming information with others is a very strong reason that we as Humans cannot remain at peace for very long. If the people in our immediate surroundings are not at peace, i.e. our home, work place, communities, etc… Our attempts at prolonged peace will be in vain as well as the happiness that we seek (happiness is a very important part of life).

So, if you wish to obtain a degree of peace that lasts over extended periods of time, you have to make one of your rules of the game (remember you make the rules) to assist others in the greater virtues of being at peace. Virtues such as love, compassion, and nurturing ensures the spread of peace which limits us being surrounded by people filled with hate, ignorance, and the Seven Deadly Sins that currently plague our earthly existence.

Otherwise, no matter if you are the richest man in the world, the happiest homemaker, or a religious leader of the biggest church in town — disruptions to your peace will be frequent. Trust me; you do not want to be surrounded by non-peaceful people. Not even if they are in another country, from other races, religions, a small child, or a stranger. Anyone can bring your peace crashing down to the gutter. Remember that all things are connected, so do your part for others and save YOURSELF.

Peace/Enlightenment only happens when we help people with the opportunity to be free of ignorance in order to experience Peace for themselves. Ignorance of oneself is the greatest danger to human life, the most powerful weapon of mass destruction to anyone or any country. There is no real happiness without Peace. A guaranteed outcome of humans not being at peace is disastrous on so many different levels i.e. failed relationships, criminal activities, terrorism, etc… Look at these threatening phenomena for yourself.

AWARENESS

Be aware that once you entered into worldly existence, the world is changed forever. To what extent you have shaped our world remains to be seen, but the impact is profound and absolute. You are extraordinary, a living creature formed from non-living, non-thinking, raw material. You are physically capable of giving and receiving love the only privileged being in the trillions of years of cosmic existence that is capable of doing so. Now don't you feel special? You should because you are.

Scientific Rule of Thumb:

<u>Form follows Function.</u> In other words the structure of an object is generally made to serve certain functions. For example, a hammer's shape is made for pounding nails and pulling them out. A giraffe's long neck was created to eat the leaves of tall trees. Its form follows its function.

This rule is pretty clear but I have never seen this rule applied to enlightenment.

"X's" Scientific Rule of Thumb:

<u>Form follows Enlightenment.</u> A Horse is a magnificent animal beautiful, majestic, and durable. Its form definitely follows its function. They're fast and have incredible endurance, but "Why can't they read or write?"

The Supreme Being in all of its wisdom will not place the intellectual brain capacity of a human in a form that cannot utilize its intellectual birthright to its full potential. Say for instance that you have a horse with the intellectual brain capability of an Albert Einstein. Now look at its body. It has hooves instead of hands so it can't write down its thoughts. The horse can't speak because its vocal cords can't formulate words. It would be imprisoned inside its own body; therefore its reasoning must be limited. If you were that horse with a human brain life would not be very fun would it? That would be beyond all mortal cruelty. Humans bodies were intentionally designed to have virtually unlimited learning potential. This is the basis of awareness.

Many of us waste this potential, ignore this potential, or deprive people of their true potential because of their social status. Humans often serve to be the cruelest creatures of them all.

> The brain is like a muscle. When we think well, we feel good. Understanding is a kind of ecstasy.
> – *Carl Sagan*
>
> Ignorance imposed, knowingly or unknowingly is evil.
> – *"X"*

"What is Awareness?"

Self-Awareness is our greatest attribute as well as our greatest curse. Why? The only thing that separates us from any of God's creatures, including apes, is that we are aware of what we are capable of in the scheme of things. If a chimpanzee had self-awareness, it would be driving a BMW or Lexus lecturing on economics using sign language and writing to communicate. The chimpanzee would be able to figure out what its average lifespan is, what it could make with its hands, and how food and exercise could affect its health.

The better your self-awareness the greater the understanding of all things is open for your contemplation. The curse of this is that we can reason with ourselves, often to the point of depression and self-harm. Where other creatures have an immutable state of structure and rules, with reflex actions governing their existence, we humans do not. Only humans have the capability of living a non-structured life and therefore constantly consciously transform our present existence.

Case in Point:

Have you ever heard a dog complaining about its hair looking awful? Or, saying "I'm too fat." "I don't like ham because it's too salty." "I need to build bigger muscles." Reader if you have heard a dog speak of these things, dial your local phone operator and make a reservation for the nearest mental health facility. Ultimate self-awareness comes to human beings when we realize that we are the superior "organic computers" on earth. We are living "computers" and we can reason and create what we want our lives to be.

COMPUTERS: All living things are computers to some degree.

Case in Point:

You, as a human being, can only determine what you are by the life experiences you have had. When you were born, you had very little life experience. Therefore, when you were an infant, your brain or "computer memory" was very small. There was very little perceived thought in your brain to define who or what you are. As an infant, all that is in your programming is simple response. The rest is formed as data stored in your blossoming brain computer. This data is to be used as a future knowledge base to be accessed at your command, given that you have a healthy capacity to retrieve it.

Another Case in Point:

If you take a French baby and place it in the United States to develop in a family where all five people speak a different language (no French), and ensure that each person interacts with the baby daily, the baby's brand new blank "computer" brain will download all the different interactions and the baby will begin to learn all the languages it has had contact with, except French. Being French by birth means nothing. Language is acquired by exposure to other human beings. This exposure and exchange of language could also be named "interactive programming." If the

French baby had remained in France, it would naturally download the French language and cultural experiences, and the baby would become French and no doubt a future wine connoisseur.

On the other hand, limiting or extinguishing human contact with an infant has proven disastrous. The computer is nothing without programming, so the very survival of the baby is at risk. We human beings are living, breathing, walking, talking, computer-generated realities. We learn our beliefs, disbeliefs, what we think we know about others and ourselves from what we experience. Then we recreate and recycle all of our past experiences every second of every day for the rest of our lives. You are a wonderful biological computer with the ability to create and understand.

You have the capability to tweak and manipulate both your own programming and the programming of other human beings.

Be proud, endlessly proud, that you are the best computer ever created and much more.

Be proud that you are playing the grandest game ever created, and that *you* are the source of that game.

PSYCHOTHERAPY

I submit that the reason that a lot of therapy programs fail to get permanent, lasting results is because therapy deals with you as *whom* you are, not *what* you are. *What* you are is a computer, programmed for likes and dislikes. The programs are set from very early life and remain the same because you are a program that is self-defining. *Who* you are is a being full of stresses, emotions, and personality, inside a moveable body. The *What* can never be gotten rid of, but the *Who* can be improved by recognizing that you have the power to choose and create your life.

Ignoring what you perceive as "bad" impulses is not the way to go. Acknowledge the impulse within yourself, and if you feel comfortable, communicate and share with someone else the reality of the *impulses* that you feel. In the truthful sharing with another human (preferably a non-judgmental friend), there is a freedom to create another scenario than the one you are experiencing when you feel the "bad" impulses. Allow yourself to let go of how hard you want to be on yourself. If you apply yourself to this principle and practice, you can create greater control over your own mental programming.

> To have courage for whatever comes in life -
> everything lies in that.
> *– Mother Teresa*
>
> We don't see things as they are, we see them as we are.
> *– Anais Nin*
>
> You have no friends; you have no enemies;
> you have only teachers.
> *– Ancient Saying*

PERSONALITY

Walkin' Personality, Talkin' Personality, Smilin' Personality…

The Story of Three Cavemen:

When the Supreme Being and all of its wisdom created our animal skin and designer-loin-cloth wearing, cave dwelling ancestors it had to have a fail-safe way to ensure their survival over the ages. Being that the world was a much more savage environment in those days, it served mankind best to be a little different in regards to personality traits.

Enter Caveman #1, Caveman #2, and Caveman #3 our ancestors.

Caveman #1 is a risk taking personality. Caveman #2 is a cautionary personality (a combination of risk taker and non-risk taker). Caveman #3 is a non-risk taking personality.

Looking for a new shelter from the icy elements they stumble upon a dark inviting cave and of course there is nothing a Caveman likes more than a big beautiful cave. It's the condo of its day.

Caveman #1 (the risk taker) says, "I'm going in to check out the cave to see if it's safe, has a suitable toilet, and a natural hot tub. Who's coming with me?"

Caveman #3 (the non-risk taker) quickly shouts, "Fool are you crazy! I'm not going anywhere near that cave. You can count me out! Heck no, no way man!"

Caveman #2 (the cautionary Personality, part risk and part non-risk) says "Hey man. I'll go to the mouth of the cave and throw rocks if you get cornered, but I'm not going in."

So Caveman #1 ventures deep into the dark cave all alone as Caveman #3 waits at the cave opening keeping a lookout. Caveman# 2 stands a good 50 feet away outside the cave entrance. All of the sudden a horrific blood curdling scream is heard. Caveman #3 standing by the cave entrance quickly runs inside the cave and shouts, "Its Caveman #2! The King Kong of the Cave Bears is out there eating that coward alive! Let's get out of here!"

The risk taking Caveman and the cautionary Caveman live on to become our venerable ancestors; their differences in personality helped to ensure our survival. By the way, if you haven't already guessed by reading the book thus far, I'm a risk taking personality. I must inform you that no personality is better than the next; all can be equally successful in life. They are just different in their approach.

The moral of the story is figure out what personality you were born with. If you're a risk taker (the first kid to explore or start trouble) like me, use that to your advantage. I'm not saying be stupid and throw all caution to the wind but you may want to look at positive ways to express this in your work and in your play. Negative ways are starting fights and arguments with anyone you come in contact with especially if they don't fit into your risk-taking bravado-filled world.

If you're a non-risk taker, (never tried anything as a kid unless it's proven safe) invest in things that are more concrete and less risky including personal relationships and money ventures. Negative ways include passive aggressive behavior and letting other people take all the risk for you.

If you're a cautionary personality, (follow around the older kids and did as they told but sometimes wary) and you closely investigate life itself. Don't always take what people say as the gospel truth. You tend to make great scientists and investigators. Negative ways include procrastination and thinking that life owes you something just for surviving.

Please, please remember through enlightenment and positive action you can transcend even your natal personality (the personality you're born with) so rise up to the challenge and be a powerful force in this life.

> Life's a play; all the world's a stage; and you're the star!
> – *William Shakespeare - adapted*

"What is Personality?"

Personality is part birthright (genetics), determined by sexual identification, and whether you are a risk-taking computer program, a non-risk taking computer program, or a cautionary computer program (a mixture of the previous two).

Perceived "good" or "bad" lifetime experience plays a tremendous part of what constitutes our personality which includes environments, race compartmentalization (belief that you are different from others because of your race), health status, physical appearance (pretty, ugly, etc…) optimism/pessimism, and whatever else one might wish to apply to the origin of ones personality.

You think that this is who you are – but it is NOT.

Personality is the thing that you present to others while playing the Game of Life. Given the proper focus and commitment to releasing yourself from bitter past experiences you can transform what you have considered your "personality" into a completely different one if that is what you choose.

When I say "transform" your personality I am referring to traumatic experiences we had at a very young age resulting in the development of what we consider to be our "personality identification". This causes us to believe that life just has certain things that we can't break away from in our personal lives. Traumatic experiences tend to repeat in different situations over and over again throughout our lives keeping our established self-defining personality in place and this is why many of us feel "stuck" in our lives. For example, "I can't get a good job because… I can't have that girl because… I can't lose weight because… I can't trust anyone because… and so on."

Even at a very young age, when you make the choices that create your personality, you are making a conscious effort to do so. Transformation/creation is always a choice for Human Beings. Generally in youth, personalities are tweaked for survival.

Case In Point:

I had three very traumatic personal life experiences that altered the way my program functions and guides my life (these awful experiences use to guide my life fully but not anymore). Everyone has at least three or more starting from early childhood (make a list of your top traumatic experiences).

Traumatic Experience #1
At the bright young age of three, I remember seeing my mother and father having a terrible argument. I also remember that I was too young to understand what all the fussing was about. My lovely mother was ironing clothing at the time and my father in a drunken fit of rage grabbed the iron and tried to burn mother in her beautiful face. Thank God that mother was able to fend him off without getting burned. The next thing I remember was the police coming into our home with bright lights flashing outside and my dad packing his bags never to live with us again.

Traumatic Experience #2
At the age of twelve I had my first girlfriend who was fifteen at the time and much taller than me and very attractive I must say. She taught me how to french kiss (kissing with a little tongue action) and sometimes we would do it for several minutes at a time in private. One day two of my cousins ventured around the back of my house and saw me kissing my tall girlfriend. I had to tiptoe to do it and they teased me relentlessly about it for days. I had to break up with her to stop the teasing; it broke my little heart. To this day she is still the best kisser I ever had.

Traumatic Experience #3

I was fourteen years old and still a virgin so to be accepted by the guys I reluctantly had sex with a girl I did not know to be accepted by my friends. I didn't even know what to do and I didn't enjoy it at all but I pretended I did so that I wouldn't be teased and called a sissy.

Now let's examine the effects these three experiences had on my life.

#1 After the horrifying fight between mother and father and his consequential removal from my young life, I figured that I had to be cunning and strategic to prevent myself from suffering future harm and to look to other men for fatherly love. Just in case you were wondering, my mother and I have long since forgiven my father and we all have caring, loving relationships.

#2 The incessant teasing by my older, but still youthful cousins, about the kissing caused me to become extremely shy and quiet around women. I felt that my interactions with them would cause me embarrassment or rejection.

#3 This chain of events caused me to develop objectification of women by seeing them as sex objects and a means of having important status among my male counterparts. Thankfully I chose to pursue the path of spiritual enlightenment and after 8 years of self imposed celibacy, I began to see women as the wonderful beings that they are – my intellectual equals and the builders of families, the glue that binds civilizations, and beloved and trustworthy friends, sisters, mothers, grandmothers, aunts, cousins, wives and everyone a beauty queen through-in-through.

Can you not see how traumatic experiences guide our everyday lives throughout our lives, and sometimes I really wish they didn't. The purpose of the choices you made in youth – to do what it seemed must be done – was in order to survive the unforeseeable situations you found yourself in at that time.

You can continue to let the circumstances and difficulties / challenges of your life continue to be perceptibly unbearable and suffer, or transform your personality to save yourself a life-long smorgasbord of grief right now. That is the powerful being you really are. Either way, you have a choice. Everything that you do in life, no matter how selfish or unselfish it may seem, is, in fact, done for your own satisfaction. Whether you do something bad to someone or something so seemingly unselfishly good for someone, you really are just doing it for yourself. This is part of all living creatures' hardwiring – the mechanism that makes you feel satisfaction. Therefore, you can be good to me all you want and *cash* is a favorite gift of mine if your interested.

It is understanding what you are, what makes you tick, what is it about yourself that causes you to make the choices that you make that is of grave importance – the rest gives education, positive support, acknowledgement, and the positive creative process of repetition with one's self-programming, affords you the chance to transform and play the game of life with hearty conviction. In other words you are a computer that can add to its present existing program to make itself better, less stressed out, smarter, and less likely to be someone's fool because you fully understand your state of being and make up the rules of how you play the game of life.

"Ready to free yourself from the prison that is your mind?" try this on for size. It's enlightening, fat-free, and entertaining.

Look back at your life and see where you made up your mind that your personality was fixed and would always be a certain way. It could be comprised of many things – for example, shyness / independence, fearfulness / bravery, narcissism / self-loathing, domination / submission, unworthiness / superiority, insecurity / soundness, etc.

You can perceive all of these qualities as good or bad. Locate those traits that you see are preventing you from living a productive life.

Write them down and figure out what effects these ways of thinking are having in your life. Generally, a good way to locate them is to look at your personal intimate relationships or friendships past and present. i.e. Boyfriend / Girlfriend, Wife / Husband, Life Partner / Life Partner, Parent / Child, Friend/Friend etc… the good stuff.

What things keep showing up as complaints in your relationships, either about yourself or the other people involved? Discuss what you see with someone you trust and are close to, acknowledge the issues/traits you see. Look at different ways of relating in your relationships with loved one's and see what shows up. (Even if you don't think there is not a snowball's chance in Heck that this will happen!) Try it and see what opens up for you in regards to having healthy *peaceful* relationships.

Let's get a few things straight right now people. No one, not even God, is responsible for your happiness, you are. It does not matter how old you are. Whether you are one or one hundred you are the gatekeeper of your happiness/peace. So stop being a baby and use your freedom of choice to make it happen. If you wallow in pity and self-loathing, and you think that everything you think, do, and say is right, you're wrong! Idiotically wrong. So Kids stop blaming your Parents, Parents stop blaming your Kids, everybody stop blaming anybody and promote some peace in your world instead of expecting someone else to do it for you. Life simply does not work that way.

Personality "problems" take on a life of their own when you look at them, so be patient. Staying with the identification process of traumatic experiences will decrease negative influences on you. So be diligent and keep up the important work you are doing to be a light for the world or for yourself at least. Don't be a lazy good for nothing idiot.

By the way, the talking that goes on in your head as you are reading this book – like whether you like it, agree/disagree with what I write, whether the words are good or bad, etc. that voice – it is not who you are. The voice that reacts in an abundance of emotional ways is not you. It is just talking inside your head. The talking in your head is part of your created personality, and it runs your life. It runs your life by providing an underlying conversation that lives from innuendo, half-truths, assumptions, insecurities, and sometimes even downright crazy talk.

So hear the talking in your head, acknowledge that it is there talking all the time, and dismiss it in favor of what you have chosen to be important in your life. Most of the talking in your head is not needed and stops you from doing what you need to do to have a great life. If you are listening to it (by the way we always are), find the facts and only the facts in what the talking is saying. Even more important identify the untruths it tends to focus on and realize that it is just assumptions. Ignore it if it stops you from being productive with your life. Negative assumptions only have a place in scientific experiments otherwise they destroy your life.

FOLLOW-UP QUESTION:

"If the talking that goes on inside my head causes so many problems why is it there in the first place?"

Good question Sherlock. The talking in the head is paramount in the intellectual evolution of human beings. Without it, we would still be simple-minded cave dwellers playing the Game of Life in a far less grand and marvelous way. Our basic brain/mind computer program is geared towards survival. If the talking in the head were not there to give us assumptions, speculations, second guesses, and reasonable probabilities, we would be operating within a set/static program similar to most other organisms on the planet.

Case in Point:

Chimpanzees, apes, dolphins, whales, parakeets, and some other animals have high level intelligence systems for certain types of information built into their programming. They can be taught and learn tasks and perform tricks through repetition and reward. They can imitate and even communicate a little. However, because their level of self-awareness is so low, they fail to apply their acquired behaviors to become independently able to formulate and play games using communication. Ergo, it can be said that they fail to grasp or initiate any true spoken "language."

Language, as defined by Webster's, is "(a) The human use of voice sounds, and often of written symbols that represent these sounds, in organized combinations or patterns to express and communicate thoughts and feelings. (b) A system of words formed from such combinations and patterns, used by a group of human beings with a shared history or set of traditions."

Animals as brilliant as they are can only function within the limits of their programming. They do not have the capacity for developing language or have the ability to think separately in their heads (i.e. *"the talking in the head"* that we humans have). This inability to split their consciousness and see themselves as separate from present reality to a possible future reality completes the distinction of what it is to be human.

"The talking in the head" is a renegade program, the Ghost in our computer the part of thinking that gives us the precious gift of choice. The freedom to choose regardless of circumstances or our past experience is a uniquely human phenomenon. If not for this renegade program of choice, there would be no possibility present for us to "think outside the box." Thinking outside the box simply would not occur because our existence would be limited to the box (like other less intellectual animals). Life would occur for us as it does for animals, simply by what happens, moment-to-moment, unconcerned with future advancements in life and science. Life would be a continuous, ceaseless flow in one direction, a linear experience like most men's attitudes when they have to go shopping with their wives or girlfriends.

Always acknowledge a fault. This will throw those in authority off their guard and give you an opportunity to commit more.
– Mark Twain

EMOTIONS

"I love you."
"I hate you!"
"Please, forgive me?"
"I didn't like you that much anyway!"
"I can't help myself."

All in one short, heated conversation.

Emotion (Webster's) (from Old French *esmovoir* to excite, Latin *exmovere,* to move outward, *ex* – outward: *movere* – to move.) 1. a. a complex, usually strong, subjective response, as love or fear. b. such a response, involving physiological changes such as a preparation for action. 3. the part of the consciousness that involves feeling or sensibility.

"What are Emotions??"

Emotions could also be called your personality traits acted out in an inner, more private form (feelings), or in an outer more public manner (expressions). Because people think their personality is who they are, and because emotions are associated with the personality, people assume that their emotions are the bulk of what we are. Emotions attach themselves to the talking inside your head. Actually, the emotions and the personality are NOT who we really are. Examine the following statement usually uttered by an overly emotional state of being in a person called "anger" "I can't help myself!" When you speak in language, in that moment in time you are what you say you are most of the time. When we make statements like, "I can't help myself!" we have chosen to give control of our life to a negative emotion rather than give ourselves over to positive emotions that serve a better purpose. We "cop out" and give ourselves over to some emotional state that is familiar to us in our past life situational programming.

When you ride the emotional roller coaster devoid of emotional control, you are definitely headed in the wrong direction, a direction that takes you away from what you truly are committed to being in life. Emotions can and must be controlled. As Human Beings we must experience emotions as they jump into our mental sphere of awareness, but we should realize the place they hold in our lives. By allowing emotions to rise and fall away like the goo' in a lava lamp, we become our own worst enemy. The ancient Egyptians had a saying, "When you let emotions takeover your life you let a snake wear your King or Queen's crown on its head," which means that you let the worst qualities of your mind rule over the best qualities of your mind that signifies true royalty among humankind. It's a fool's game to hold on to negative emotions, it's the main detriment to our life's peaceful purpose. You can easily become masterful over negative emotions with practice over time.

Case in Point:

"I want ice cream! I want it right now!" A child having a temper tantrum, screaming to the top of its' lungs can quickly be swayed to end the seemingly uncontrollable outburst by offering them their favorite treat and it ends as quickly as it started.

"I can't help myself!" So are you saying that you do not have more control over your emotions than a little child?

You do have emotional control right now if you so choose to exercise it. Sure, all of us have the immediate initial onslaught of the myriad of negative emotions that inhabit our brain/mind program. Just recognize it, acknowledge that it is there, and choose a more functional positive emotion. It works the same way as when we give a child their favorite treat, only you picture your "treat" as peace of mind, stable relationships, health, longevity, and happiness. I would take that over ice cream any time – almost anytime.

EMOTIONS

It is an immutable scientific fact that whenever you have negative emotional responses you have the exact negative emotional responses that you placed upon similar negative circumstances as a child. In fact the present state of all your emotional responses is completely (*child like*) virtually all the time. The age of the response is only varied by the age of the child you are being at the time of your perceived unwanted predicaments.

We live out our daily existences in different immature stages of strongly rooted past experiences. You are a computer program and the programming started from day one. As children we start out and as children we remain forever. Sorry kids. Now you see why the world's governments are so terrible. They are all run by the same greedy pre-schoolers who refused to share their candy and gloated over the fact that you didn't have any.

The great thing about being a perpetual child is that when you are really enjoying life you are at your most childish. No matter how old you are, you are being a kid again – only the toys are a little higher tech. Men love shiny cars and motor bikes, women love beautifying their hair, men love sports, and women love shoes. Think about the cuteness off it all. Makes you want to say ahhhh doesn't it. Children your parents are kids like you only in bigger bodies with more financial responsibilities. Parents have purposely taken on tough responsibilities to ensure the continuation of our noble species so cut them some slack why don't you.

All emotions are not negative, of course. The following are the ones that make life worth living: Joy, excitement, compassion, relatedness, and so on. Choose emotions that make you smile, and share those with the world. The choice to be happy is there at any time and it is an inexhaustible resource. So be happy.

Forgiving Past Transgressions:

> The weak can never forgive. Forgiveness is an attribute of the strong.
> – *Mahatma Gandhi*

> He who forgiveth, and is reconciled unto his enemy, shall receive his reward from God, for he loveth not the unjust doers.
> – *The Koran*

> Be it known unto you therefore, men and brethren, that through this man is preached unto you the forgiveness of sins.
> – *The Holy Bible Act 13:38*

> If your life is not all you want it to be, it may be that you have some forgiving to do!
> – *Unknown*

I'm not saying that you are not to be moved by the terrors of the world but if you don't forgive negative energy will eventually engulf and eat away at you causing destruction to yourself. Pent-up anger, frustration, and hatred engulfing your life negatively becomes an excuse for your failures and mistreatment of others usually years after the offending culprit is long gone and out of the picture called your life. Thinking about past abuses and hating your abusers will not physically harm the perpetrator of the offense so that wish is an empty one. Forgiveness is not for the offender; it's for you. During the creation of your act of forgiveness you leave the realm of childhood and in an instant catapult yourself into adulthood. There is nothing childish in forgiveness; it is the remover of anguish and a pathway to salvation.

If you will look at how not forgiving keeps you trapped in the past your suffering will be lifelong and you will cause other innocents around you to suffer because that kind of pain always demands a sacrifice. So who will it be, your best friend, your family members, your co-workers, your children, or yourself? Pick them out now while you're reading this book. It may sound silly but that is what you do subconsciously (automatically) everyday. What is the REWARD in that?

Free yourself from that negative energy stream and trust in the wisdom of God that allows you to keep feeling and breathing. It is a scientific fact that negative energy and positive energy can't inhabit the same space at the same time. I personally can testify to the cleansing power of forgiveness. If not for that fact, you would not be reading this book right now.

> When angry, count ten before you speak, if very angry, a hundred.
> – *Thomas Jefferson*

Lets all practice controlling our emotions including the author known as "X". Practice, practice, practice!

Emotional Control Exercise:

Step #1 Stop being a child for a moment and concentrate a minute.

Step #2 Write down all of the things that immediately come to mind that make you angry, frustrated, sad, or anxious.

Example: My list, the "X" list if you will.

- Ignorant people who refuse to for whatever reason get some education about life and themselves. (This excludes you of course because you paid for this book. Thanks. If you did not pay you are a bootlegger, or a cheapskate, and borrowed this book from someone. (If that is the case, add yourself back to list #1 – just kidding.)

- People who cut me off in traffic. (I know it seems petty but I'm still human.)

- People who are late all the time and always have some lame excuse for doing it. (Uh oohh. I think I just made my own list.)

Etc., etc... you get the point - whatever comes to mind.

Step #3 Now that you have your list asks these questions about each of them.

   a. What is the REWARD? (From now on for the rest of your life be brave enough to take the time to honestly ask and answer this question. If the reward stinks you have made a stupid choice and fix that as soon as it is possible.)

   b. What does it do to promote peace in this world?

   c. Why don't I feel guilty about this negative behavior?

   d. Why do I feel guilty about this negative behavior?

   e. Where does it come from? (I.e. negative childhood experiences, drug abuse, sexually repressed desires, religious beliefs, family practices, or cultural bias.)

   f. If this is part of my program how can I control it without repressing it? (Look for healthy outlets and/or support groups to work things out.)

Step #4 Discuss your findings with yourself first and if you feel comfortable discuss these findings with a non-judgmental confidant. How do you know if they are non-judgmental? Ask them if they will be judgmental and if they say yes find someone else. One way to be more assured that they are what they say they are is to invite the confidant to write out a list and participate in the exercise with you. If their negative emotional list is not juicy enough they are probably not being forthright. Thank them for their time, kick them to the curb and move on. Don't be deterred; your well-being and peace of mind is at stake and the universe will find a way to aid you in your search for peace and happiness I promise you. The more you share yourself with others who will listen without judgment to your growing understanding of yourself, the greater the control you will gain over your destiny and emotions. This greatly increases your chances to be a positive contributor to humanity and I will be so proud of you as well as those who love you. Are you still breathing? If not take a deep breathe and continue reading.

Step #5 FORGIVENESS – THE MOST IMPORTANT KEY

Forgiveness is the most important part of controlling your emotions simply because it releases you from your internal suffering and in-turn lessens your ability to hate instead of love. The act of forgiveness is the only thing that can free you completely of negative emotions and stops the vengeful cycle of harmful overly selfish physical and verbal reactions. Not forgiving is to push away the people you love and care about locking away your divine celestial beauty in a blockade of emotional anguish imprisoned in your spirit possibly for eternity.

"How can I forgive when I could never do it before?"

How to forgive is not as hard as we make it out to be it is unnecessarily harder than it has to be when you let the hurtful childish emotions dictate your adult actions. Just realize that forgiving will vanquish a lifetime of suffering if you do it without vengeance and hatred. If you *can* communicate with the people you have to forgive don't be fearful, don't cope out, don't worry, and don't have expectations of what the other person's reaction will be. Force yourself to do it anyway, be strong. If you *can't* reach the people you need talk to too forgive ask God to help you forgive them and God will help if you are sincere in the asking. Let God/Supreme Being be your guide and councilor.

Be brave and make a list of all the people who have ever wronged you in anyway your entire life starting from childhood to present day. If you were like me you may need two blank sheets of paper. *Remember forgiveness is for you to free yourself.* Contact them face-to-face or by phone, whichever you are more comfortable with but do it now or as close to now as possible.

FORGIVNESS LIST – People to Forgive (Past/Present/Deceased)

1. Immediate Family – The Source Of Your Life and Beginning Stages of Your Programming. **THE MOST IMPORTANT TO FORGIVE.** If you can't start with forgiveness with your Immediate Family I promise you if you need to forgive them and you do not your suffering will never end and you can discontinue the forgiveness exercise right here.

    - Immediate Family List – Mothers/Fathers, Brothers/Sisters, Grandmothers/Grandfathers, Husband/Wife, Children

2. Non-Immediate Family

    - Uncles/Aunts, Cousins

3. Friends

    - Best Friends, Acquaintances, Co-workers, Peers

4. Lovers' (past and present), Ex-lovers, Boyfriends / Girlfriends

e. Enemies – Usually the hardest people to forgive. Enemies are sick people who have violated you in the worst way physically, mentally, or sexually. If you never talk to someone you trust implicitly or a professional councilor about past abuses by enemies so that you can forgive them you will never be truly happy and other innocents will suffer at your hands because suppressing trauma filled emotions only work to cause them to fester like an open wound. If you need help here to forgive seek professional help please.

f. Self-Forgiveness – Oftentimes we can forgive others and neglect to forgive ourselves. Usually when you have been a victim (and we all have) you also do things to lash out and become the perpetrator of negative behavior toward others. This is a terrible thing because how can you be happy engulfed in self-loathing. To err is human, mistakes are made so we can learn from life so stop being so hard on yourself and filled with regrets, it will not serve you for the better so please stop it.

> A Prayer for Self-Forgiveness:
>
> Almighty God the creator of all things. I humbly ask you to please give me the strength, love, courage, and wisdom to know that I am not perfect and that I will make mistakes, but I must not let my mistakes destroy my life and my love for my fellow man. Help me to help myself so that I can help others to know courage, love, and peace. Thank you for giving me the gift of life. Please forgive me.

Clean the slate of your life and start anew with positivism and power not being the victim ever again. Feel the weight of the world removed from your spirit and truly live brothers and sisters. To forgive opens the way for true Power, Sanity, Love, Life, and Happiness.

For Pete's sake do the exercise because it really will help. This is a scientific and spiritual fact.

> If you are unhappy, you are too high up in your mind.
> – *Carl Jung*

SURVIVAL

"I am not going in that cave it might be dangerous!"

… "If we don't get rain soon, or find water, we won't make it…"

Ask yourself these two questions:

1. Are you a survivor?
2. Are you good at the game of survival?

If you answered yes to these questions – congratulations! You are one of many who think they have accomplished a great thing in their life. "But is this really so?" Let me tell you a secret. No living thing wins at the game of survival, because death is always guaranteed. Therefore it is impossible to win at the game of survival. But you can win at the game of life. Deal with life by living it to its fullest potential. Stop worrying about survival all the time. Whether the time of your death is now or a hundred years from now, it will bring about the end of your earthly life. "Popcorn anyone?" so live now because now is all we have.

> Taking life seriously is interesting; not taking life seriously is a lot of fun.
> – "X"

> What if this is as good as it gets?
> – Jack Nicholson - Movie - As Good as it Gets

What is Survival?

Survival is base level programming built into all living organisms that works to ensure its continued life expectancy with as little *discomfort* as possible for as long as it can live.

Case in Point:

"Don't you get a little upset when someone is trying to kill you?"

End point.

SURVIVAL

Our survival "programming" can oftentimes be put into overdrive in people suffering great amounts of fear, great amounts of depression, or great amounts of unjust social treatment and oppression. Desperate people are extremely dangerous to themselves and to others. People who override the survival program by hate are more dangerous still. Life completely loses any value for those individuals that perceive someone or something to be the cause of their fiery hatred. Terrorists are generally people who have been harshly oppressed in some way and may have experienced harsh social economic inequality, have physical and mental anguishes forced upon them, and perhaps engaged in war/wars that was totally unjust in its actions and reasoning tend to warp their beliefs about the beauty to be enjoyed in life.

> When an eighteen-year-old Palestinian girl is induced to blow herself up, and in the process kills a seventeen-year-old Israeli girl, the future itself is dying.
> – George W. Bush - USA Commander and Chief

Case in Point:

Suicide bombers who feel they have wrongfully suffered severe political oppression, severe grief at the loss of loved ones, abject hatred and rage over their livelihoods being taken away may actually think that giving their life and taking as many of their enemies lives with them is the only possible option left in order for them to have peace. Think about this for a moment. Place your self inside that desperate person's shoes. The amount of suffering he/she is presently in is unimaginable, dead to the world already with no hope of there being a better world for themselves, their children, their wives and husbands, no way to feed their sickly elderly mothers and fathers, grandmothers and grandfathers, and the only option left is a big BOOM in a one minute television spot by some attractive smiling glassy eyed reporter on some 24 hour news station.

The fact of the matter is if you were that man, woman, or child suicide bomber, placed in the same situation with the same belief system you would voluntarily go BOOM. This is the danger that is being bred in our world by hatred and ignorance every day, brothers and sisters. Think about it. If we do not promote peace, love, and understanding in the world, "Who will?"

> From now on it is only through conscious choice and through deliberate policy that humanity can survive.
> *– Pope John Paul II*

DEATH

What is Death?

There are two things certain in life. We have all heard the cliché about death and taxes.

"Death the eternal! Death the Grim Reaper!"

A murderer, sitting in the electric chair, was about to be executed.

"Have you any last requests?" asked the Warden.

"Yes," replied the murderer. "Will you hold my hand?"

Death is neither grim nor eternal. Not living your life while breath is in your body is grim. If you read previously in the chapter on Energy/Matter, all things are everlasting death is merely a transition from one state of being to the next state of being.

> I realize now how precious each day is.
> – Coach Jim Valvano – As he was dying of cancer.

Once death happens, you don't hurt that thing known as pain is in living tissue only and so is paying taxes. Sure the person you used to be, at least the form of the person you used to be may be missed, but you are not dead. Truly all deceased people are not dead, and their energy/matter still mingles with all things because all things are of all things. So live your life, be fruitful, and do not fear what is part of life and living. It is the other side of the coin. Thinking always on some level about the "end" as in "the end is coming for me – someday", does make life a more interesting game, albeit a constrained one.

Keep in mind also that life is not a dressed rehearsal. When this round is over, it is time to take the old dirt nap. This moment is it for all of us. There is only now. So all of you cheapskates who owe me money pay-up, and for the people I owe, I will pay you with the money they owe me.

> Do not be too eager to deal in death and judgment. Even the very wise cannot see all ends.
> – *Gandalf The Gray - Movie - The Lord of the Rings*

> Famous Last Words:
> Friends applaud, the comedy is over.
> – *Ludwig van Beethoven*

> First I was dying to finish high school and start college.
>
> And then I was dying to finish college and start working.
>
> And then I was dying to marry and have children.
>
> And then I was dying for my children to grow old enough so I could return to work.
>
> And then I was dying to retire.
>
> And now, I'm dying…and suddenly I realize I forgot to live.
> – *Unknown*

> Death is not the greatest loss in life. The greatest loss is what dies inside of us while we live.
> – *Norman Cousins*

> To live in hearts we leave behind is not to die.
> – *Thomas Campbell*

FEAR

Maker of wars and strife... Peace killer. Slayer of millions and prognosticator of the words, "Do these pants make me look fat??" or "Am I balding on top??"

> You gain strength, courage, and confidence by every experience in which you really stop to look fear in the face. You must do the thing which you think you cannot do.
> – *Eleanor Roosevelt*

Fear has many functions, which can be interpreted as good and bad. Fear stops children from running into the street and being struck by a car. Fear keeps the country of China from dropping an atomic bomb on the United States. Fear also works in insidious ways to stifle and kill the fun and excitement right out of living. It's a scientific fact that more people state they would rather die than speak in front of a large audience. I can honestly say I get very nervous, and have a stomach full of butterflies when I speak in front of a large audience. The heck with facing a firing squad over it! Give me the microphone Master of Ceremonies!

What is Fear?

Fear is the largest part of the survival program that is instilled in every human being on the planet. We are born into fear to keep us in survival long enough to play the game of life and propagate the species.

Granted, sometimes fear goes beyond its original programmed value to determine our very lives for us. Instead of our living our lives, fear lives our lives for us. By this, I mean that at the deepest level of our identities, fear runs the show. We are not in control – fear does the controlling.

> He who fears he will suffer, already suffers from his fear.
> – *Michel de Montaigne*
>
> The few real evils of the moment can be either cured or endured; it is only countless imaginary evils in the future that make people anxiety-ridden for a lifetime.
> – *Earl Nightingale*
>
> Be of good cheer. Do not be afraid.
> – *Jesus of Nazareth*

In order for you to win at the game of life, you must confront your fear programming. Not just once, but also many, many times a day. First, you must recognize the fear that is actually there. Investigate your fears bravely and confront them at every turn. If and when you are sure that the fear is completely gone just know that is a lie; it will return again. You can overcome your fears enough to put them in the background but they will always be a part of your life. The presence of fear is always with us, and can only be unmasked through facing it from now until the end of our days on earth.

People generally fear what they do not understand. Also, people fear being lonely, rejection, losing jobs, security, societal organizations, family members, peers, institutional rejection, other races, opposite sex, bugs, snakes, etc.

Not one of the above-listed fears is a real immediate death imposing threat. Not one of them will destroy you instantly. Yet we live as if they do. If we turn and face the fears, they will dissolve enough so they don't disrupt our lives. Otherwise we float about in our lives inside a cheesy Machiavellian illusion over and over again.

There are reasons for fearing things that may be valid because of past circumstances, but if you let them rule your life you will be very lacking in the peace department. This I can assure you. Also, those physical sensations that accompany fear are just that (i.e., tightening of the chest muscles, shortness of breath, butterflies in the stomach, etc.). They are just sensations in your physical body sending you adrenaline just in case you have to high-tail-it to the nearest hill or foxhole and these sensations will not kill you and it will pass in time. (Even though it seems like the nagging tightness in your chest and tummy will never stop). Examine and study your fears. Confront your fears. I'm not saying jump out of perfectly good airplanes but if you stop pursuing your dreams because of fear, then life will end for you on a sour note.

Fear Control Exercise:

1. Write down your fears and find out why you have them, and what is keeping them in place. A lot of times the only thing holding your fears in place is your laziness to do something about it, or that you will look silly or vulnerable if someone was to find out about them.

2. Discuss the fears with yourself and right them down. If you feel comfortable doing so, discuss your fears with someone you trust, and receive encouragement. Do so and your path to greatness and peace will give you the fortitude to live an extraordinary life. Most of the time if you attempt to face your fear alone it seems like life itself becomes unbearable. Don't let your fear of sharing your fears stop you from receiving the help, love, and stress relief you deserve.

I personally want you and everyone whom you encounter to be happy and at peace. Only you can create your life. Only you can transform the life you have into the life you are meant for. Create and transform your life into one that makes you light up and makes you want to jump out of bed every day with gratitude. Do so with the knowledge that your life and the life of your loved ones depends on this process, and this commitment.

As I mentioned earlier, studies have shown that people say their fear of speaking in front of a crowd of people is greater than their fear of death. I say to you, do not let your fear cripple your life and your living. Press on and discover a confidence and a power you have never experienced before. Be the true leader and hero of your life.

RELATIONSHIPS

A Story of "X":

I, "X", was in love with a very lovely and beautiful young lady. We had our differences like any other couple but for the most part we got along ok. Nearly 3 years to the day we began our relationship, she stole me away to a secluded area and I was hoping this was another one of her exiting amorous advances but it suddenly went sour. With tears in her mesmerizing beautiful big brown-eyes, she told me that she had been unfaithful to me and that she had unprotected sex and contracted genital herpes and, "I think I may have passed them on to you." Needlessly to say I was outraged to tears and the first thing I said to her was, "Damn! At least when I cheated on you I wore protection!" Unfortunately a visit to the local health department confirmed I had the love-bug and I thank heavens it wasn't AIDS or some other ghastly one celled creature waiting to call my body its home, but it easily could have been.

The word relationships; is defined as "being connected or associated, especially harmoniously." Relationships come in all different forms, crossing human, animal, and plant boundaries.

Psychology 101:

When you are in an intimate committed relationship the other person is never the problem, you are, so the solution to failed relationships begins with looking at your on dirty laundry and removing the mental baggage of fear, jealously, insecurity, and selfishness.

"What is a Relationship?"

A relationship is a given, connective bond between two or more beings, in which one or more of the beings involved accept and acknowledge the others' existence. The state of relationships is often interpreted differently depending on what is involved in the relating. The state of a relationship can therefore be considered "bad" or "good" depending on how those involved perceive the relationship.

For me "X", personal relationships can tend to be a bit challenging, but for you I know it is a piece of cake.

A woman applying for a job at a lemon farm was at her interview.

Interviewer – Miss do you have any actual experience when it comes to picking lemons?

Woman – As a matter of fact I do I have been married three times.

Man and wife, father and daughter, boss and employee, etc., are examples of just a few of the hundreds, even thousands of relationships present in our daily interactions. The great thing about this vast number of relationships is that you as a human being are given the opportunity to be a beacon of peace or an instrument of harm in your relationships at any given point in time. The choice is yours and therefore the union present in relationships is a very powerful thing. Given the opportunity, ask people's opinions about how they perceive your relationship with them. This gives you a glimpse, just a glimmer, of how much power you actually wield in this world. Truly, we are nothing outside of what we are in our relationships.

The creation of the world community is built on relationships. We, as humans ally ourselves with people in relationships that give us a higher probability of having and maintaining the presence of peace in our lives. In other words we try to surround ourselves with people who make us happy. Given that every living thing in nature transforms, relationships are no exception. Keep your relationships a priority in your life – really devote time and energy into nurturing healthy relationships that are meaningful to your life. Also do not be afraid to develop new relationships; this will make a profound difference for you and for the world.

Personal relationships are a valuable learning experience for all human beings because the way in which you deal with the challenges of personal relationships is largely a function of how you deal with your entire life. I.e. if you are standoffish in your personal relationships, it's a guarantee you will be standoffish in other areas of your life. Especially focus on those aspects within your personal relationships that frustrate or anger you. Those places are always a space from which to look to allow meaningful insight to occur, lifting your relationships to a higher level of intimacy and peace. So examine all of your close relationships from time to time, and reflect on how your relationship issues correlate to other problems you deal with in life as an individual. What is the REWARD?

All relationships are an ongoing life "experiment" with a meaningful, continuous process even unto death, with death being the most pleasing ultimate result. Don't freak out! The - in other words - explanation is about to show up. In other words (see, I told you), we look at being together until death do us part as the ultimate goal a measure of success for a long term committed relationship. (Unless you have an enormous life insurance policy on your partner; in that case you will take death on a short-term basis.) Just making it entertaining people!

Sex is an important part of intimate relationships but overall it plays a very small role in the success of lasting relationships. At best, "How many hours of the day do you participate physically in sexual activity?" 1, 2, 3 hours. There are still 21 or more hours left in the day. Sex-based relationships don't last because sex can't continue 24 hours a day. (What can continue every hour, every minute, of every day, is commitment, respect, integrity, and honor, the only true building blocks of caring relationships.) If you love someone the only major difference in all binding intimate relationships is that you sleep with one and not the other universally love is the same thing – acceptance.

Deceit rarely has a positive effect in any relationship, especially a relationship of marriage or lifelong partnership. So whether you chose to have one mate or one hundred, be truthful and forthcoming from the initial stages of the relationship. I have learned from personal experience that honesty from the beginning is less stressful and less hurtful to you and your mate. This approach plays a more positive note in the grander schemes of the Game of Life. Playing the game of telling him/her what they want to hear to get whatever you want (mainly sex) will not promote the kind of peace you wish to manifest in your life. All this deceit makes you look cheap and perverted in the eyes of others and it's tough to maintain peace inside an unforgiving environment.

What is the REWARD?

> My toughest fight was with my first wife.
> – *Muhammad Ali*

In case you're wondering about the lovely brown-eyed girl who passed on the herpes simplex II virus to your masterful author, I forgave her because I was being deceitful with her about my sexual activity as well. Forgiveness is very freeing and empowering, and even though - the talking in my head - said "hate her, don't forgive her, don't tell anyone you got it they will make fun of you and not accept you," I chose not to listen to it and found that people understand and it has never affected the quality of any of my intimate relationships because people really do respect honesty in relationships especially where health is concerned. Even though I parted ways with the brown-eyed girl intimately we are still good friends. If I were to put a positive spin on this passing event, and I do, I would say that I am wiser, honest, non-deceptive, and wear protection during sex every single time because we all deserve the respect to not have ailments thrust upon us without warning. If I can show you and the world my dirty laundry you can at least be protected and honest with the people in your private personal relationships.

> The only thing that I would ask of anyone is honesty.
> – "X"

LOVE

> Without friends no one would choose to live, though he had all other goods.
> – *Aristotle*

> I only want to see you laughing in the purple rain.
> – *Prince*

> Don't believe your friends when they ask you to be honest with them. All they really want is to be maintained in the good opinion they have of themselves.
> – *Albert Camus*

Love, Love, Love! What a grand and splendid thing love is. The experience of love is so inspirational that many people consider it to be the true meaning of life. So to live life without it is considered repugnant and meaningless. Many people consider life, love, and peace to be inseparable. Poets immortalize it, musicians' dwell inside of it, and everyone desires to possess it.

Love as a thought, or ideal, is beautifully romantic; but alas, love is a separate entity in and of itself.

"What is Love?"

Books tell us that the definition of "love" is: "an intense affection for another person, based on personal or familial ties." The definition goes on for some time, including all concepts of family and sexual love, love as a feeling, and the mercy and benevolence from God.

Simply put, love is the capability of one living being to have a true and unconditional acceptance of another human being regardless of race, gender, creed, age, sexual identity, or national origin. Love can also traverse from humans to other species. Love does not mean you will not have disagreements. Human beings experience disagreements more often than not but it is possible to fully accept others and ourselves, as what we are, flaws and all.

"Have you ever been the new kid on the block or in the neighborhood?" "Do you remember the tension you felt on your first day of school?" "Did you ever go from one school to another school and feel like you had to start your life all over again?" "Do you feel the awkwardness of beginning a new job?" "Do you still get nervous in the pursuit of personal intimate companionship?"

"Why do changes like these bother us so much?" "Why is there less stress when forming non-intimate friendships?"

Because instinctually we know that if we are not accepted by our new peers and *accepted* quickly our happy/peaceful life in the world is limited. If you are not accepted, you have no life because there is no one around to share life with. This is why as young children, teenagers, young adults, and senior adults, we literally bend over backwards to find out the rules of engagement and association with family and friends so that we will be accepted and fit in. The reason why it is easier to "just be friends" is because you don't have to negotiate terms for intimate sexual interactions.

No fitting in = no Life folks.

> To be no part of any body, is to be nothing.
> – John Donne

> I don't know the key to success, but the key to failure is trying to please everybody.
> – Bill Cosby

There are five stages of acceptance / love that people go through. Let's examine this phenomenon more closely shall we? First we must pick a suitable subject. "Hey you! Reading this book! You will do." See if you can see the correlation of this scientific look in the life cycle of a Human Being.

The Stages of Human Acceptance

<u>Infancy</u> (0 to 2 years old). There you are a cute little baby. The only thing you have going for you is your ability to smile, make some noise, and that cute thing. You hope that the people around you will accept you enough so that you won't get eaten or placed in a dumpster. (Scientists theorize that offspring cuteness is there so that the parents will like the baby in spite of its selfish demands for food and diaper changes. There are no coincidences in the universe.)

<u>Early Childhood Stage</u> (3 to 9 years of age). Thank heavens you have been successfully accepted by your caretakers enough to survive your most vulnerable stage, infancy. Now that you can venture out beyond the slow paced infant stage, you can explore and seek out more acceptances from similar children and other less familiar adults. Everything is going fine on your treasure hunt for acceptance until you meet other boys, girls, and adults who let you know that they can't accept you for different reasons.

Reasons like: "You're stingy with your toys and candy!" "You talk too much!" "Stop playing around!" "You're ugly!" "You're fat!" "Your cloths look funny!" "You talk funny!" "I don't like you any more!" "You're a wimp!" "You throw like a baby girl!"

You can continue to fill in the blanks.

Then you realize that there's more to this acceptance thing than you thought. Now I have to strategize with my child's brain to keep enough acceptances so that I can feel loved by people. Yet you do not have the mental capacity to figure out and realize this acceptance thing is love. You just continue to live life clueless to this fact. Negotiations, assumptions, and conjecture from your childhood shape your brain / computer program and you will live by that hardwiring for the rest of your life. Sorry, it's like that for everyone. Let the games begin.

<u>Adolescent/Teen Stage</u> (10 to 20 years of age). Now you think you have figured out everything about your life but you really haven't. That my friend is called the, "I'm so smart because I don't know that I'm an idiot stage." This gives rise to the time honored clichés: *Youth is wasted on the young and Hind site is twenty – twenty.* By the way if you are currently living your life in this stage, no hard feelings. I'm just doing my job. Also congratulations!!! You are educating yourself towards a powerful life and pulling life towards you instead of chasing it. "So are we still friends?" "Do you accept me?"

Now that you are little older and can move around in the big bad world, meeting more people of all different shapes, sizes, colors, cultures, likes, dislikes, religions, economic status, so on and so on. There are more acceptances to be had or not had, couple the natural desire to find love/acceptance with others and the onslaught of puberty (crazy, sexy, turbo charged hormones) and you have the makings of one very interesting, exciting, and problematic game.

[Enter Peer Pressure]

Even if the peer pressure game can nearly destroy you or get you killed outright, you are still compelled to play forsaking common sense and the love of people who already accept you as you are (i.e. mothers, fathers, and true friends), to be loyally involved with the hip crowd who only accepts you as the way they want you to be. That's just the way it is. So you go along with the in-crowd. Dressing alike, walking, talking, and joking alike. You think you are being a true individual because you're more like your age group and not like the older or younger age groups. NOT! You're an imitation of those you wish to immolate and impress. Adolescents and Teens are for the most part are *professional imitators.*

I'm not saying that imitation is bad or good; it's just what it is. Since you have to play the game of life for life, it would be smart to make beneficial choices that enhance your youthful lives. Pick brilliant people to imitate, and use whatever pertinent resources at hand to better yourself. The opportunities available to you in life become painfully limited if you don't make productive choices and fewer choices because people despise/dislike you socially will probably cause possible lifelong economical short-comings (no money) equal more problems than it has to be my teenage friends.

Hind site is twenty – twenty. "What is the REWARD of being part of the in-crowd?" Being part of the in-crowd got my 19-year-old Godson a lead bullet in the chest and a pine box suite. He's dead after only nine months of running hard with the hip bad-boy crowd. His actions rewarded him with Death and his family and true friends a lifetime of grief. His 4-year-old sister still doesn't understand why he's not around anymore. Stupid choices equal stupid consequences my friends sometimes permanently.

<u>Adult Stage</u> (21 to 55 years of age). Have you ever noticed that for some adults the older they get the more childish they get. That's because adults live their lives in a mature body but their minds are still in the first three stages of acceptance. To truly be an adult (which it is not necessary to be all of the time), you have to come to grips with a few things.

1. Stop lying to your friends and loved ones. It's not worth the loss of time and energy to back-up lies. I know that sometimes it tends to make you look good (for the moment) and keeps you in the good graces of acceptance (for the moment). Yet we know when or if we get caught lying we have got to pay the piper. Friends and loved ones are not the enemy. But they will be if you keep deceiving them. What is the REWARD?

2. Have INTEGRITY at all times in your life. Live your word. Give your word only if you mean to keep it. I am not saying that sometimes situations will not arise to

make keeping your word a distinct improbability. Just be responsible with your actions after the fact and straighten it out.

3. Always seek out ways to educate yourself on the pathway to peace, enlightenment, and enjoyment of life. That's all it takes to be an adult. Be a kid the rest of the time and have a rip-roaring good time.

<u>Mature Adult</u> (56 to infinity years of age). Holly cow!!! You have made it to an age undreamed of by our Caveman ancestors (they rarely lived past 33 years old). So my learned friends, "Have you found enlightenment yet?" If your answer is maybe, that's a no. If your answer is "yes," that's a fib. If your answer is "no," that's the right answer.

The answer is "no" because enlightenment is never a constant. Enlightenment is the precursor for peace and peace only exists by passing it on to the next person and you do that by simply sharing knowledge and volunteering a helping hand to those less fortunate. Enlightenment is a fantasy unless you apply this principle every day of your life. You may live in a home for assisted living, a retirement home, or home alone. This world still needs you to do what you were sent here for and that is to keep making a difference in people's lives. The alternative is to be treated like over grown babies, be bored stiff, and to have very limited acceptance or love in your life. It's never too late to make a difference in the world even if it's not with your biological family. Regain your dignity and salvation in the service of mankind. You guys have the best music and all the knowledge in the world. Live a little.

Don't let the bastards grind you down!
– *General Joseph W. Stillwell*

Hatred does not cease through hatred at any time. Hatred ceases through love. This is an unalterable law.
– *Buddha*

Love = Acceptance; Nothing more - Nothing less.

Behold If You Will…

THE HISTORY OF ROMANCE

Romance did not begin as the whimsical course of action that it is today. In the ancient times of the hunter-gatherer, the men being mostly brawn rather than brain had to go out into the wilderness to hunt and bring home the bacon to provide for their mate/mates at the risk of being eaten alive, freezing to death, being dehydrated, having other men raid their homes and steal their families, or facing some other unforeseen tragedy. The women who stayed behind and cared for themselves and the children (I'm sure some women hunted sometimes as well), waited with doubtful thoughts unsure that the family men would return home alive with loads of tasty groceries. As you can imagine these were very harrowing times. When the men made it home with the goods, to ensure life would be sustained another day, this was a time of great relief, jubilation, and full tummies.

As time passed and ancient civilizations sprang up around the world. Greater material goods needed to be provided by the men for the safety and comforts of their women as modernization of societies occurred. For the desert nomadic people water, goats, and camels were the crowd pleasers, for the people in Iceland warm housing and large loads of fish were prized, for jungle people wild boar and beautiful birds' feathers brightened the day. The people began to live long enough to be elders and they said, "Hey men we have to survive too!" which eventually led to the creation of dowries among the tribes of humankind (a dowry is necessary predetermined gifts to trade to a family to marry their daughter).

Eventually humans became very successful with raising livestock and building shelters and this led to the development of cities and governments. This raised the stakes of what people needed to maintain a happy home. If you were a Prince and you wanted to marry a Princess, you would have to provide a huge dowry showing that you had enough money and power to be considered an equal among your peers. Large dowries meant that you could provide for the Princess and her family if need be and dowries became a long-standing custom for many members of society's social classes.

Presently in western civilizations, instead of accumulating dowries we desperately try to fill our bank accounts, drive fancy cars, wear designer clothes, get manicures and pedicures, buy bling-bling jewelry, eat at the most expensive restaurants, and even get PhD's to present them to our potential mates along with the occasional candy and flower combo.

To sum it up: Romance is an unspoken promise that men will be able to provide for their mates / wives / girlfriends desirable goods whatever those may be. Gratifying women's every want and need even if discomfort, great hardship, or sacrifice of life and limb acquiring the cherished goods is involved. It goes all the way back to the giddy feeling our lovely lady ancestors had when they knew that they were not going to starve to death thanks to those brave men. Nowadays men focus most of their energy and resources towards the accumulation of material wealth because the rich guys generally get the prettiest women. This can and often does leave a void for honor, respect, and loyalty to be included in the mix.

SEX

Is love, sex? Is sex, love?

How often have we heard the term, "making love" used to describe the sexual act? "Making love" as a term is misleading because it is certainly possible to separate the two words more so than to keep them together in that phrase. You can definitely love someone without having sex with him or her; and you can also definitely have sex with someone outside of the presence of love. Love cannot be made or manufactured. I know of no formula in any science that can cause one human being to unconditionally accept another, without reservation.

> Masturbation has never given anybody an STD. It's never gotten any girl pregnant, and it's never made anybody go crazy, and you always know you're having sex with somebody you love.
> – Jocelyn Elders - former U.S. Surgeon General

"What is Sex?"

Sex is a biological, physical, mechanical function of the body that creates a pleasurable stimulus to one or more beings. Sex can be experienced either jointly or separately for the purpose of pleasure, the purpose of procreation, or both.

Every human being has pleasure stimulus buttons present in the programming of his/her physical body. Sexual functioning of the body is available for transformation. What stimulates you sexually stimulates you and you alone, but the things that cause your sexual triggers (what turns you on) can be transformed by you a lot of the time if you wish it so.

Social norms and taboos, cultural body manipulations (plastic surgeries), body height and size, and the subjective evaluation by others of the overall pleasantness of the general physical appearance of the body and personality influence what is considered to be sexually desirable or pleasurable.

Sex, like Fear, is a direct part of the *survival programming* of human beings. The brain/body impulses which are linked to the survival programs are constantly present and cannot be turned on and off at will.

Therefore, the sexual drive in humans is continuous, and has to be monitored and "kept in check" once the drive is awakened electro-chemically during puberty. Self-imposed programming, the use of conscientious choice versus vague impulsive decision can assist human beings in guiding and regulating their reaction to the sex drive of their physical body. In other words, you can choose when and how you want to have sex, but to think you can stop the desire to have sex is foolhardy.

It is not wise or even advisable to attempt to "turn off" the sexual drive, as this will likely result in a terrible battle in which a human usually does not emerge victorious, at least without unpleasant consequence. Such fighting with the body would also result in the termination of human beings as a species since the sex drive exists to perpetuate the species.

So, denying sex to an organism as aware as human beings would serve only to frustrate and mislead them. Education and information about the realities of sex should be available to all young people transitioning into adult life. Adult human beings who grasp the balance of interplay within the body and soul of people should be consulted and used as a resource for young people. This can prevent a lot of the painful lessons learned after the fact by taking the mystery out of the sexual act and empowering the youths by giving them the precious gift of deeper self-awareness.

Diversity of sexual activity is the norm for modern humans and can differ greatly from person to person, culture to culture.

"Whatever floats your boat" is the motto of sexual desire. A "normal" sexual appetite is then left up to the participants' discretion and interpretations. However, with self-awareness as a guide, people are more than up to the job of having responsible and amazing sexual expression. Sex can create and destroy lives, so please, educate yourself in order to receive the best results from your sexual experiences.

If you are going to float the sexual boat, take the helm and be the captain of your destiny. Please do not crash your boat off of a raging sky-scrapper waterfall of foaming animal sexual desire. Get tested for STD's and treated if you have to. Stop unwanted pregnancies and nip them in the bud. Abstinence is good but sex is great and even with abstinence programs in place upwards to 90% of teenagers still explores the sexual waters (in America – this may vary country to country). So if you have sex boys and girls, wear protection.

Parents please stop turning a blind eye to the sexual desires of your children. Educate them please. I know that it is hard to give your babies permission to discuss their sexual lives without scaring the life out of them but clearly see the alternatives. Not discussing sex with your kids oftentimes leads them into ignorance and there's nothing a sexual predator loves more than curious innocent kids. Dads, don't put all of the tough discussions about sex on the mothers. Be included in these talks even with your daughters. Positive male input is invaluable in these matters because males will get females pregnant. Life partners and guardians, do the same for your kids as well. You are the best defense in an offensive world of opportunistic sex hounds.

Kids, if your parents are being babies take it upon yourselves to have a discussion with them about sex. This will show those stuffy adults that you are a responsible young adult. This will force them to see that you are not a powerless little kid and that you are brilliant and committed to having a fantastic life. (Doing this is bound to get you the car keys from time to time or maybe even some wheels of your own). Being adult in the education of the innocents, (not excluding kids and parents), is a pathway to enlightenment, and a valuable tool in the promotion of peace.

TRUTH

"Do you, <u>state your name</u>, solemnly swear to tell the truth, the whole truth, and nothing but the truth, so help you God????"

If I only had a nickel for every time someone lied behind the guise of that statement!

"Is it human to lie and to lie often?"

The Story of the Cute Little Girl Who Fibbed:

Once there was the cutest little girl in the world just barely beginning to use her cute power of speech. Her equally beautiful mother had just finished baking some hot and gooey organic chocolate chip cookies and takes them out of the oven. The cute little girl smelled the hot batch of cookies and couldn't resist asking her mother for one. Mother said, "Not before dinner sweetheart."

This of course infuriated the cutest little girl in the world and as soon as her mom leaves the kitchen the little girl snatched three cookies and gobbled them all up. Mother came back to the scene of the crime and noticed that some of the cookies were missing. "What happened to the cookies?" mother asked the little girl. The cute little girl had never taken cookies before without her mother's permission so she quickly came up with a brilliant idea. "Mama a little birdie ate the cookies and flew out the window," exclaimed the cute little girl. Mother just looks at her and giggles and says, "I hope the cookies don't ruin the birdie's appetite for dinner," then she walked away. The cute little girl had just figured out that being a deceitful liar could save one's backside. "Is it human to lie?" Yes it is.

We all begin to tell untruths on our own because our survival program felt that it was being threatened. The cute little girl never had anyone teach her to lie. No one walked up to her when her mom wasn't around and said, "Hey, cute little girl, if one day your mother ever bakes some chocolate chip cookies and she doesn't give you some, lie through your frigg'in teeth." It's only natural to deceive to save yourself. As daunting as this seems, to realize people are masters of deceit and to continue to get in there and keep on swinging is mighty inspirational. It is simple, yet mind-boggling. Lying is all fun and games for a while, but when the truth is found there will be heck to pay.

[Curiosity Piece]

Deceit (which is another form of a lie) is prevalent throughout the animal kingdom. One of my favorite examples of trickery is the Angler Fish. The Angler Fish is so deviously clever that it has developed an appendage over its head that looks like a distressed wiggle worm. When an unsuspecting hungry little fish thinks it has come upon an easy meal and gets to close to the mouth of the Angler Fish, it becomes an instant sushi meal for the tricky fish only with no wasabi. See if you can find other examples in nature of ways that animals deceive.

"What is the Truth?"

Truth is universal by nature, factual, based in reality, and is indisputable. Things are either so or not so. That is it. Easy enough – the truth is the truth, except when it is not. Then it is something else. Not Truth.

TRUTH

It was Russian leader Vladimir Lenin, the late ruler of the former Soviet Union who stated, "A lie told often enough becomes the truth." This speaks to the phenomenon of the absolute creative power of human language.

> Men willingly believe what they wish.
> – Julius Caesar

Some people lie so chronically that their lies literally become the truth. Truth is true only when you personally believe that it is true. Also, the truth we speak may be true because we are unaware of some other facts, which would make what we think is the truth, in fact, untrue. In that case, again, the lie becomes truth upon our mental ownership of it, regardless of the additional unknown facts. The more we become aware of something, the more understanding of the truth we can have and experience. Thus, whatever you have experienced is the truth to you/or a lie to you unless you prove it to yourself otherwise.

There have been many people in the past that challenged the status quo by taking it upon themselves to investigate the existing laws of the land for what is true, spurred on by whatever motives, justifications, and explanations they may have had at the time of their investigation into the matter. When the truth is discovered and revealed to the unsuspecting average man/woman/citizen, the person revealing this truth will be met in one of several different ways:

1. Complete acceptance and joy!
   (Best case scenario, and highly improbable)
2. Disbelief
3. Ridicule
4. Anger
5. Violence

6. Shock / Ostracism (getting kicked out of something)
7. Murder / Death (worst case)

If the bearer of this new truth persists, and if he/she is backed with irrefutable physical proof, scientific evidence, or psychological support, the truth will ultimately be accepted and acknowledged as truth. If the truth is not accepted by the masses because of religious, scientific, or moral constraints, the bearer of the truth may be burned alive at the stake, "Anyone for roasted marshmallows?"

Always, Always, Always, seek the truth. Like I said before no book, institution, or dogma, is the know it all end all. I challenge you to do the research yourself whenever possible about your own life. You may even write a book even better than mine. Though I very seriously doubt that my friend. Just kidding! Your awareness of the truth is the salvation of the ever-transforming world. The world is not flat anymore, but it sure used to be! And that was considered the truth!

Now for the Wise Elder Tidbit:

A wise elder once told me lying is a bad thing, but there is a time when lying is a good thing. It's a good thing when someone will use the truth that you convey to destroy you, or anyone, or anything that you may care about. It is ok to lie to your enemy. It would be stupid to tell them the Truth. Lie to your enemies if you must, and feel no guilt.

"What's the real benefit of telling the truth?"

Telling the truth establishes rapport and trust with the very people that give greater meaning to our lives and establishes your value as a decent man or woman of your word.

> You do ill if you praise, but worse if your censure, what you do not understand.
> – *Leonardo da Vinci*

COMMUNICATION

> A word fitly spoken is like apples of gold in pictures of silver.
> – *Proverbs 25:11*

Behold the awesome power of communication! Some scientists believe that the female of the Human species invented verbal communication. Now whatever made them come to that conclusion? Hummm…

Humans love communication. We use it all the time, all of our lives. If we stop communicating, we die. Communication enables the game of life to be played on the highest levels of sentient beings' comprehension. Being that humans are computers, the only way we gather our data is through the many forms of transferable communication.

"What is Communication?"

Human communication has two forms: verbal and physical.

Verbal includes the words we think in our heads, the words we speak, other sounds we make, as well as reading words. Words hold our thoughts and allow them to be expressed to many other people. Words connect us soul to soul. Physical communication includes body language, hand signals, the physical act of writing, and all physical actions or other forms of nonverbal communication.

The use of a floating bone in the throat called the hyoid and the voice box called the larynx, work together to produce sound and form it into complex patterns called words. Sounds are made in the form of vibrations, and are interpreted by other human beings as meaningful speech. Verbal communication is very powerful because the thoughts it provokes can inspire us to either be great in life or to fail in life and that is pretty powerful stuff my friend. You perceive who you are, and what you are, by the thoughts you have translated into words and/or speech. Everything that you are, and know yourself to be or to become comes about through the process of human communication.

You are identified as *whom* you are by how other human beings communicate to you *what* you are. Repeatedly calling someone negative or "bad" names will eventually cause him/her to become as your communication calls him/her a lot of the time. I.e. "you're stupid, you will never amount to anything, you never listen." Unless positive communication intervenes, he/she will become encompassed with negative thoughts. So be sure to introduce positive words into the world to inspire and create beautiful people. This one important action promotes the spread of peace.

Physical communication is done willingly or subconsciously by the body you live in. Even though body language is understated, it is equally or more important than verbal communication. Human beings convey who they are, who you are for them, what they want and need, and their likes and dislikes, all through *verbal* communication, but to be manifested in a physical form, physical actions must take place to be physically communicated. According to scientific studies by law enforcement organizations nearly 100% of the time when the mind is purposely being deceitful the body of the deceitful person will react in subtle negative ways. In this manner the interrogator interviewing the suspect picks up on body movements with a trained eye and in the process finagles confessions from guilty parties because they unknowingly give themselves away by their physical body language.

COMMUNICATION

Case in Point:

If you are married, and your spouse/significant other tells you that they love you, then proceed to immediately punch you in the eye, it would seem that they are not being honest in their communication with you. On the other hand if he/she gently kisses you, you have no confusion about the message they are giving you. So deliver clear verbal and physical communication to ensure that the message you wish to send is what is coming across to those you communicate with. It is totally impossible for communication of any kind to fail to cause some kind of mental effect on human beings. All communication carries within it the power of intent. Even a little two-letter word like "Hi" accompanied by tone, speed of vocal delivery, and the physical look on your face can convey very powerful intent. Communication is that powerful.

Communication literally identifies who you are in the world. As I said earlier in the book, we are the experience of God. The Supreme Being experiences physical life through us. In turn other peoples' communications about you is the expression of *you* in the world.

Case in Point:

Let's say that I take a beautiful smiling head-shot picture of you, my dear reader, and place it in your favorite local newspaper, and right above your picture reads the following caption;

Famous scientist discovers a cure for cancer.

Or

Meet the next President of the United States.

Or

Winner of the persimmon pie-eating contest for 3 years running.

Or

Murdered entire family with a shoestring and a lucky horseshoe.

You get the picture. None of this is true but to someone who does not know you personally and has never heard a different conversation about you, "that is you!" You my friend are only the conversations that family, friends, and strangers have about you in the world (it defines every stitch of you even in your own mind believe it or not). Now behold the awesome power of the communicative Media television, gossip papers, newspapers, radio, books, magazines, computers, and big-mouthed people. (Believe me the Media clearly knows the power they wield with their forms of communication. Just look at their bank accounts.)

Now you can really see why celebrities get into such a huff about the gossip about them. They constantly have to defend who they are based on what is being communicated about them in the world of human melodrama. True or False jabs about your character is indeed one of the highest prices of fame. That's the reason I can't stand to be around people who gossip – most of the time. Sorry, sometimes inquiring minds want to know. So I can't tell you enough the critical importance communication is to your success within the existence of your world. Master communication. It is a tool that came bring you a better world or you can become a slave to it and live in a crummy world. The choice is yours.

HEALTH

"I'm as healthy as an ox!" "I'm going to live to be a hundred!" "I can party all night!"

> The greatest wealth is health.
> – Virgil

"What is Health?"

Health is the ability of an organic organism to maintain its functionality without severe disruptions or threats to its existence. Harmful causes range from disease, trauma, stress, harmful environmental elements, toxic chemicals, and the natural process of aging. The better your health is, the more easily you can cope with the problems encountered in the game of life.

> Health is a state of complete physical, mental, and social wellbeing, and not merely the absence of disease and infirmity.
> – World Health Organization

Basically, the human body is a flesh-covered chemistry set governed by chemical and electrical functions. The body requires water, chemical and metal compounds, along with exercise and massage, to keep it at optimal fitness. Like any chemistry set, the introduction of the wrong chemicals or inadequate chemical levels can create problems for the body. If you want to be fully happy in life, you need a body that is up to the challenge.

The Health Care Industry is a money-making giant, number one worldwide in cash accumulation. "Why is that?" A lot of countries have free health care, but I digress.

Your body requires vitamins, minerals, proteins, and carbohydrates (either from vegetables or meats), along with essential fatty acids. Adequate amounts of exercise and physical exertion are required to maintain muscle mass and tone, support heart/cardiac health, and bone density (thickness).

Vitamins and minerals boost the immune system, build tissue and bone, and help maintain proper chemical-electrical flow. The lack of one vitamin or mineral in your diet can cause over 500 different diseases as proven by noble prizewinning scientist Dr. Joel Wallach.

Fruits, vegetables, proteins, and complex carbohydrates build muscle and maintain and create fuels for the body to keep it mobile and agile.

Essential fatty Acids - (EFA's) ensure the proper functioning of your brain-computer. Essential Fatty Acids cover the outer layer of every cell of the internal body's organs. Sources of Omega 3 and Omega 6 from flax seed, olive oil (extra virgin is best), and fish oil are crucial for healthy organ development and maintenance; this slows down or prevents clogged blood vessels.

The human body is made up almost completely of water. Therefore, a human being can survive for two months plus without food, but only three to five days without water. Do the math – water is life – neglect hydration at your own risk. Water consumption has been found in scientific studies to reduce heart attacks, aid in weight loss, keep muscles from tearing and spasms, boost the immune system, and improve brain memory function. Water there is no substitute.

Advice from Master Massage Therapist and Author "X":

[The Story of the Hip That Nearly Destroyed Me]

I, "X", was a massage client long before I became a Master Massage Therapist. One day I woke up from a sound sleep at the young age of *young age*. (Age is not really that important to the story). I had this tremendous amount of shooting pain in my right hip and this pain got worse and worse over a two-year period. Eventually the pain got so bad that I couldn't sit down and my right leg would literally buckle out from underneath me. So I finally I had to go see the Doctor. The Doctor told me that I had Sciatica, a debilitating condition of the Gluteus (butt muscles) and he gave me painkillers and muscle relaxing drugs. This worked for a couple of days but after that the pain returned and I stayed near comatose for most of the day, which is not good for a working man. I told the Doc I could not afford to continue to stay drugged up so he sent me to physical therapy.

Two weeks of daily physical therapy and ultra sound treatments on my hip and the pain still plagued me as if it were an evil little clown teasing me. My sessions ended with the physical therapist and my only option was to take more drugs and suffer, or just suffer. I nearly gave up all thoughts of being helped until I meet this beautiful saintly massage therapist in line with me at the post office. We made small talk and I told her about my hip problem. She suggested that I should come see her and I said I would because she was pretty darn cute. It was a life changing decision. After just 3 massage treatments the pain was gone and I can walk, run, and sit down for weeks typing this lovely story for you. Massage works. I promise you.

Massage is the world's greatest all-natural stress reliever and it is a scientific fact that no drug can relieve stress as well as the human touch. Scientists estimate that up to 85% of diseases are brought on by stress and that high amounts of stress can cause as much damage to your body as smoking two packs of cigarettes a day, mainly due to the massive amounts of the hormone cortisol that becomes deadly to the body causing them to be stored in fat cells which leads to excess fat production and creating more problems mentally and physically. Add in the multitudes of people with congenital spinal deformities (i.e. Scoliosis), accidental injuries from vehicle and other accidents, as well as collapsed spinal disc due to deterioration of the spinal column causing nerve compression/impingement (which can harm and weaken internal organs as well as muscles) adds to the agony of musculoskeletal difficulties. It is a scientific fact that as people mature in age, the muscle tissue gets harder (like a tough steak), and the cartilage and tendons get softer. As a master massage therapist that has worked on nearly 1,000 people of all backgrounds, shapes, and sizes, find that the most common cause of bodily injury is from stress and repetitive motion (using the same muscles over and over again) create painful tense muscle tissue and mental anguish.

The body is a biological vehicle and it deserves and requires maintenance like any other vehicle. Similar to the functions of a car, the human body has pumps, filters, lubrication, fuel intake, waste production, and accidents. Working out the kinks in the back, neck, shoulders, and hips can be the difference between living a happy life or a life of chronic pain and depression. Stress is powerful internalized energy that if it has no outlet for release, overwhelms its host. Stop wondering why you get sick, injured, gain weight, or suffer pain. It's STRESS!!!

People who are in pain all the time due to never having proper body maintenance (massages) may have the reward of pain as a lifelong constant companion. The legendary Bob Hope got massages nearly every day and he lived to be over 100 years old in good health and high spirits (Massage increases life expectancy). It's a proven fact that corporations that provide massages for their employees have less absenteeism at work, higher morale, fewer health insurance billings, and more productivity, which greatly increases the monetary bottom line. There is no separating of the body and mind when it comes to health. That is like saying I have a Mercedes-Benz with a go-cart engine inside. "How will it not affect the quality of the car?" Get your massages; it's not a luxury. It's a necessity for the preservation of your health.

A word from your friendly Chiropractor/Yoga Instructor:

There is an ancient yoga saying, "You are only as old as the flexibility of your spine." You are born with flexibility and not strength so from the beginning flexibility is of the greater importance and you develop strength over time. When you lose flexibility, you lose it because it's the beginning of old age. Maintain spine flexibility with chiropractic adjustments, stretches, and massages to revitalize your youthful agility.

Your health is your wealth and your measurable quality of life. Please confer with a physician before making drastic changes in diet, exercise, and other treatment areas.

When I initially wrote this chapter on health I ended it here, but as I spoke to more and more people I have come to the conclusion that people really need more pertinent health information so here it is.

Major Killers of Human Beings: (In no particular order)

1. Heart Disease (Watch your diet, exercise)
2. Diabetes (Watch your diet, exercise)
3. Cancer (Watch your diet, not to much sun, get check ups)
4. Strokes (Watch your diet)
5. Stress (Meditate, yoga, massage, alone time)
6. Drug Addiction (Counseling, medical attention)
7. Sexually Transmitted Diseases (Get tested, protection)
8. Car Accidents (Don't drive reckless, don't drink)
9. Obesity (Watch your diet, counseling, exercise)

10. Suicide (Counseling)
11. Environmental Toxins (Drink filtered water, clean Earth)
12. Accidental Deaths in Hospitals (Yes, it is a major cause of Death. Stay healthy.)
13. Murder and Involuntary Homicides.

We have lots of challenges to living and playing the game of life. Be that as it may, we are here to play the game in every capacity it takes us and health is no exclusion to this fact. I have talked to quite a few doctors in my time and I would on occasion ask them. "What would be the biggest health challenge to a maturing person?" Hands down the #1 answer is OBESITY.

Obesity is simply being overweight to a point that it becomes life threatening. It can cause virtually every one of the previously mentioned Major Killers to gain a foothold on your health.

> Life expectancy would grow by leaps and bounds if green vegetables smelled as good as bacon.
> – Doug Larson

Obesity is the fastest rising facilitator of health problems to modern humans since the plague and gangster rap. According to the laws of thermonuclear dynamics if a body takes in more fuel than a body can burn then the surplus fuel accumulates within said body. In other words, if you eat too much you get fat. Scientific studies have shown that eating fatty foods causes similar addictive effects to other addictive substances like cocaine, heroin, crystal meth, and caffeine. Fast food restaurants are also privy to this information that food addicts buy more food and make them more money. Food based addiction programs need to be developed to address this fact.

The human liver organ will manufacture *body fat* in great quantities when the interior of the human body is filled with toxins. Excess fats have two major functions to provide food for you in case you are starving and can't make it to your local fast food hub, and to store toxins to keep them from destroying your vital organs. That's why it is stored outwardly instead of inwardly and it increases your waist size. Fat speeds up the aging process and increases your chances of a problematic life of poor health and mental anguish. Seek help and education in this mater.

"What is another big culprit to our health?" – FOOD!!!

"Why is food a culprit?" "Don't we need it to live?"

Yes we do. It's the wrong foods that cause preventable problems and we all know what they are. But man!!! That junk food is tasty-riffic! What to do? You can do like a lot of my relatives and say, "God made it to eat. So as long as I pray over it and bless it, it is fine to eat. Now pass me the salt, the high blood pressure medication, and my insulin shot." From the Queen of England, to the Pope, the scientific physical laws of chemistry bind all people. If not, I would eat junk food 24 hours, 7 days a week. Intellectually I know that would not be prudent.

The reason it is so hard for people to break the cycle of obesity from parent to child and so on is because we are fast food babies born into a world of dangerously fatty Triglyceride toxicity being stuffed into our newly blossoming brain programming from the moment we can say chee-bugger. Think about it! You are given the same thing your parents eat and they say it tastes good and the great taste blended with verbal/physical communication reinforcement makes it a shoe-in that fast food will be like your mother's kitchen for the rest of your short lived poor quality of life. In order to break the cycle, you need to treat unhealthy, non-nutritional foods like illegal drugs and baby killing poisons.

You would not want those dangerous substances going into your body or your loved ones bodies so some changes need to be made around your home and limits need to be placed on unhealthy fast food and restaurant consumption. Break the cycle of death and shattered dreams. Do whatever it takes to be a healthier and happier you. If you're skinny and eat a lot of junk fast food you are at just as much risk or more as an obese person because your fat is housed deep inside your body clogging up the works.

Therefore, I am 90% vegan (no meat) and 10% dairy (cheese, no liquid milk). I'm a Lacto-vegetarian. I can honestly say that it works well for my healthy countenance and physical appearance especially in comparison to those around the same super young age group as me, still blessing the heck out of those fried meat dishes. Vegans that eat no meat or dairy must take a Vitamin B12 supplement because it is required and not found in vegetables, only meat or dairy, sorry. I'm not saying completely give up your fatty diets. Just be mindful, aware, and educated. You can become a Flex-aterian. A Flex-aterian is a person who eats mostly healthy fruits and vegetables but still occasionally eats meat as well. Modify your diets a little and give your body a break from heavy meats now and then it will thank you for it.

HEART DISEASE is any condition that makes it impossible for the heart to collect and pump blood throughout the body.

The heart is a powerful muscle about the size of a two fists (in adults) and pumps enough blood through your body to fill up a small lake everyday. Eating foods high in saturated fats and cholesterol can cause dire effects on this incredible muscle. If you have heart problems, the supplement CoQ10 (co-enzyme Q10) has been proven to help in the case of weak or enlarged heart problems. Also extra vitamin C and calcium will help to fight infection and provide fuel for the heart muscle. Most importantly stop eating fried saturated fatty foods, add healthy fats to your diet. (This will lessen the effects of clogging arteries by LDL bad fats), exercise, eat more fruits and vegetables, limit alcohol consumption, and definitely don't smoke.

DIABETES occurs when your body looses its abilities to process blood sugars from the lack of insulin. If you were not born with this affliction, more often than not your diet of saturated fats, excess carbohydrates, and simple sugar intake (candy, soda, granulated sugar, white flour) is the culprit causing this problem. What happens is that the body has organic mechanized parts like the pancreas that produces insulin in massive quantities because of your diet and like any other part in the physical world it literally burns out and breaks. If you are overweight, sometimes losing as little as ten pounds will reverse the effects of diabetes. Exercising, taking vitamin C, incorporating healthy fats into your diet to raise the level of HDL (good cholesterols) and reducing saturated fatty foods from the diet can also reverse the effects of diabetes.

STROKES happen when your blood vessels become so clogged with plaque or internal blood clots that proper oxygenated blood flow can't occur often resulting in paralysis, sever brain damage/malfunction, and death. This condition happened to my grandfather at a young age and all of my memories of him were of him being completely paralyzed on his entire left side; he was virtually a vegetable. It was not a pretty picture any way you look at it and very difficult for grandpa to play happily at the game of life. Once again stop with the fatty fried foods, eat more fruits and vegetables, brush your teeth to keep bacteria from your mouth from entering your blood stream to damage your arteries, add healthy fats to your diet, (healthy fats don't make rocky clogs of plaque and lessens the risk of blood clots breaking off of blood vessel walls), and exercise. Early warning signs of clogged arteries are losing your eyesight and male impotence. This happens because the arteries that feed these areas are small and can be the first to become clogged with plaque.

CANCERS are our own cells gone renegade and mad inside our own bodies, usually because of free radical invasion from pollutants or too much sunshine with no sun block during the hours of 12pm until 3pm. When good cells go bad, the DNA encoding goes haywire and instead of producing health happy cells to replace our old dying cells (which happens constantly your body completely reproduces every cell in its body roughly every ninety days except for brain and spinal cells which cannot be reproduced), this can cause a chain reaction which can corrupt the entire system which can lead to premature baldness, agonizing pain beyond imagination, and death. Eating a healthy diet of fruits and vegetables, limiting saturated fats, taking vitamin C, eating healthy fats, limiting sun exposure, and exercising can greatly reduce your chances of contracting cancer.

DRUG ADDICTON feels pretty darn good while you're getting high and pretty darn bad when your heart is beating so fast that it's going to explode. You're looking for acceptance and reassurance and you found it in drugs. I can't say this without a shadow of a doubt but I don't think they have drug rehab centers in the afterlife so you better kick the habit now while you still have some dignity and teeth left in your head. The number one most addictive drug in the world is "tahh dahh!" caffeine. Not as glamorous as nicotine (cigarettes, cigars, and chewing tobacco), cocaine, heroin, crystal meth, ecstasy, and weed (marijuana) but too much will damage your internal organs like the others so drink it sparingly and leave the others the heck alone. Yeah baby!

STDs (sexually transmitted diseases) range from herpes (the lovebug) to AIDS (auto immune deficiency disease is a deadly killer of millions and growing daily). Signs of infection in the private area include itching, redness, swelling, foul odor, puss emissions from the urethra (hole where urine comes out), blistering, and canker sores. Also unexplainable flu-like symptoms and fatigue can occur as well as no symptoms at all. If you have sex get tested and if you have unprotected sex put down this book and go get tested now. Be smart, safe, and wear protection (aka skins, jimmy hats, rubbers, condoms) every single time will save you a world of shame, grief, screaming babies with hungry mouths to feed, burning singed private parts (penises and vaginas), and dying with an emaciated rotting corpse body like the zombies seen in the horror movies.

Seriously, I have seen people dying from AIDS taking buckets of pills to try to stay alive from every walk of life. Starting with cute little newborn babies born with AIDS from teens to young adults, you don't want this infecting you. Wear protection each time you have sex. All it takes is one time to be exposed and it's a no win situation and you can catch some STDs from oral sex as well. Stay protected! Your privates will thank you for it.

CAR ACCIDENTS are as American as apple pie. Reckless driving, drinking, taking drugs, talking on cell phones, eating, sleeping, and looking at pretty girls often causes this vehicular mayhem to end the lives of tens of thousands every year. Please wear your seat belts; don't drink and drive, and be careful out there.

SUICIDE among teenagers has been on an alarming increase in recent years. "What is the reason for this?" "I can't rightly say," but if I were to speculate it would be the lack of power kids feel they have because peers and adults don't respect them as smart, responsible human beings. If you feel so depressed that you want to snuff out your life, please seek counseling. Losing your life over silly untrue emotions simply is not worth it.

ENVIROMENTAL TOXINS are proven to be the cause of the astronomical increase in cancer deaths worldwide. Breast, lung, prostate, colon, and skin cancer will affect nearly 1 out of 2 American citizens in their lifetime with many resulting in fatalities. Environmental toxins come from polluted water, air pollution, food pollution (i.e. dyes, preservatives, and food enhancers), hazardous household cleansers, cosmetics, deodorants, depletion of the ozone layer, factory waste byproducts, and hazardous drug use. Studies show that the United States has two times more environmental toxins than almost any other country in the world so cleaning up the environment will make the world a healthier and secure safe place to live for future innocent generations.

ACCIDENTAL HOSPITAL DEATHS account for over a whopping 100,000 dead each year in America alone nearly as much as car accidents in some years. "How does this happen?" To err is human, so if you get the wrong medication, the wrong dosage, do not receive the medicines as prescribed, get one of the many infections that float about in areas where the sick people are housed, have a piece of gauze or surgical instrument left in your body after surgery, you might just get your ticket to the other side. Personally I stay as stress free and healthy as possible or I just might wake up in the hospital like my grandfather did with his legs amputated.

MURDER AND INVOLUTARY HOMICIDE cause indescribable grief to thousands of people on a daily basis. Guns the weapon of choice strike from a distance not like the old days when you had to get your hands dirty to kill someone. I stated earlier that my Godson was murdered at age 19 and the effect on the family will last forever. People argue that if you take away guns from people this would stop the killing, but I say teach the ignorant awareness and enlightenment to stay the violent trigger finger. Gun registering, anti-gun laws, and harsher prison sentences have done absolutely noting to end skyrocketing murder rates. Education is cheaper and more feasible than building more prisons and taking away our constitutional rights.

> All we are saying is give peace a chance.
> – John Lennon

"X's" Favorite All Natural Remedies

For acne: Eat less fried food, wash your face with a non-irritating soap or use a mild facial cleanser rather than soap. Always be gentle with your facial skin, never scrub, and wash your face

2 to 3 times a day. After the face is clean, put on a greaseless facial moisturizer.

HEALTH NOTE – Whenever a cyst develops in the body, it is the way the immune system stops toxins from spreading all over the body by incasing it in fibrous sacks far away from internal organs.

For Acid Reflux: *(from Kevin Trudeau's book – "Natural Cures They Don't Want You to Know About")*

Try 1 to 2 tablespoons of apple cider vinegar before eating a heavy meal or after the meal if gassing occurs – *adapted*.

For Obesity: Drink lots of clean water, exercise, eat healthier (start out big meals with light soups when you can), and fast 2 days every change of season (winter, spring, summer, and fall). Use only fresh squeezed citrus juice and water to flush out the toxins and before starting the fast, drink a bottle of Citrate of Magnesium laxative the day before at bedtime to clean out your intestines.

HEALTH NOTE - 70% of the bodies' immune functions begins in the intestines. Remember the body is an organic vehicle and like any other vehicle needs cleaning and fine-tuning to run properly. A cleansing fast every 3 months can do the trick.

For Soar Throat: Gargle with warm salt water, followed by gargling with apple cider vinegar, then with antiseptic mouthwash for 60 seconds each, 2 to 3 times daily. Take 3000 ml of vitamin C twice a day AM and PM. **(Do not use for Strep-throat infection.)**

For Colds and Flu: Take Vitamin C 3000 ml 2 times a day, drink plenty of water, don't lie down during the day – sit up. Keep warm but don't over heat. Temperatures over 101 degrees Fahrenheit are dangerous. Eat hot soups and drink hot fluids without sugars and you can add lemon and a little honey if you like.

For Arthritis of the Joints: Take Knox Gelatin Joint repair along with liquid colloidal minerals for 2 to 3 months, (follow directions on containers). You can use chondroiten and glucosamin as well. If the cartilages inside the joints are not rheumatoid or completely deteriorated, the cartilage can be replenished. I suffered severe arthritis pain in my left knee for two years from years of jogging on hard surfaces but following the aforementioned advice I have not suffered the knee joint pain for over 14 years.

For General Overall Health: Drink lots of water (close to half your body weight in ounces). Don't get too much sun. Eat more fruits and vegetables. Exercise 3 to 4 days a week. 2-day fresh water/citrus fruit juice fast every change of season and before you start the fast drink a bottle of Citrate of Magnesium laxative to clean out your intestine the day before, right before bedtime. Get massages to relieve stress. Take a good multi-vitamin. Also take separately extra vitamin C, Calcium, and the B vitamins. Incorporate Essential Fatty Acids into you diet from time to time from raw nuts, extra virgin olive oil, fish oil, and other sources. Most importantly educate yourself on what is good and bad for you and limit your hospital visits from critical concerns to routine check-ups.

Friendly Reminder:

Consider trying out Herbal, Homeopathic, Acupuncture, and other Holistic remedies by practicing professionals in these areas and check out your local health food stores for more natural healthy alternatives. After all, most prescription drugs originally come from plant and earthen mineral deposits.

Live healthy; Love life.

DISCLAIMER

The information, remedies, and dietary suggestions presented here are not intended to replace any diagnosis or treatment by your physician, nutritionist, or health care provider. Please consult professional health care practitioners before making changes in diet and prescriptions.

> In order to make a change, you have to stand up and expose the corruption in government, and the connection between big corporations and government.
> – *Kevin Trudeau*

INTEGRITY

"What is Integrity?"

Integrity is simply your being your word making agreements and keeping them, when you said you would.

> Living with integrity means:
>
> - Not settling for less than what you know you deserve in your relationships.
>
> - Asking for what you want and need from others.
>
> - Speaking your truth, even though it might create conflict or tension.
>
> - Behaving in ways that are in harmony with your personal values.
>
> - Making choices based on what you believe, and not what others believe.
>   – *Barbara De Angelis*

You are a being of sound as well as of energy/matter, and the volume and truth of your *word* can strengthen you in this world or be your downfall.

Consider yourself in the game of life to be the most powerful player of all. If the game happens to be chess, you are the Queen as long as you keep your word with the intention of being truthful. This will ensure your sovereignty with others. If you do not keep your word, live your word, and be your word, your power will be compromised. You will become as a Pawn in the great chess game of life being treated as -less than- you are by other, more powerful chess pieces. Quite possibly, this low state of personal power will linger for the rest of your life, or at least until you give your word and keep it.

INTEGRITY

Case in Point:

You are at your job. You are a hard worker and you get along with everyone there for the most part. But every other Friday you come down with a sickness of some sort and Fridays tend to be the busiest day of the week. Your co-workers know that you just want to have three-day weekends all the time. They are not being fooled by that fake sick voice on the phone. You're no Marlon Brando (a famous actor). "How long will it be before they plot ways to get you fired from your job?" You have lost your integrity with them so watch your back.

Let's say you're a teenager and you spent your weekly allowance on video games but you want to go hang out with your friends at the movie. You know you can't ask for more loot from your parents so you sneak into their personal belongings and take money or something to pawn. Parents know most of the time when stuff is missing and if they wait to confront you after this has taken place several times you are in for it. It was just a test to measure the amount of integrity you had about yourself. Now they won't let you borrow the car so sad.

You're a beloved Public Official and you get caught doing something underhanded. You can call you career past history.

When you drop the ball with your integrity, simply stop, apologize, and make a new promise. But try to keep the promise from being unrealistic like I promise not to eat junk food again. Right! Keep it real and simple. Then follow through on your promise, thereby restoring your integrity. So, if you take on a job, give it your all. Even if you dislike the position, eventually your integrity will impact other people. They will recognize your abilities and/or you will recognize your own blossoming abilities. This realization generally increases your choices and enables you to move to a job with a more comfortable fit.

You are nothing if your word means nothing.

Honor your Word and the world will honor you.

> Through pride we are ever deceiving ourselves. But deep down below the surface of the average conscience a still, small voice says to us, "Something is out of tune."
> – *Carl Jung*

TIME

Time is…on my side.

Sometimes it seems that time is on our side, but even that illusion is short-lived.

"What is Time?"

Time is – nothing. It is a man-made concept, made up to generate the beginnings and ends of games. Time was made up to make the game of life more interesting. (Can you find other man-made concepts in the world?)

Have you ever seen a cat ask another cat, "Hey Dude! What time is it?" If it was asking a New York cat it would reply, "Time for you to get a watch!" I love New Yorkers! Cats just live out their lives, then transform to a different state of being when they leave this earthly plane.

We can exist without the concept of time, but that would hinder many of the games that we play. You would be late for work or appointments, have no birthdays to celebrate, be unable to make estimates on how long you could live, and when it is the end of Tax season. So time is a good or bad thing depending upon the effects it has on your particular game plan.

> If you are 5 minutes early for every appointment you will never be late.
> – *Herm Edwards*

> Time is infinitely more precious than money, and there is nothing common between them. You cannot accumulate time: you cannot borrow time: you can never tell how much time you have left in the Bank of Life. Time is life.
> – *Israel Davidson*

In time comes wisdom.
– George Takei - Star Trek Captain -
Words Spoken on the Howard Stern Show

PROBLEMS

> I wish I could make a happier world – harmonious, friendly and peaceful.
> – *His Holiness the Dali Lama*

"I never have enough money!" "People only like me for my money." "I hate my job!" "My parents don't understand me."

"What are Problems?"

Problems are challenges that living organism's face in life that may be harshly perceived life situations of a physical or mental nature, or both. These stressful situations create different instinctual or emotional responses, usually negative with organisms that have the capacity to identify them as such.

Are problems the bane of all creation?

The reason that the Supreme Being allows problems to exist is for us to learn from them and by doing so be transformed into more enlightened beings. Otherwise, "What would be the point of being alive and playing the game of life?" So no matter how much money you have, how enlightened you are, how nice, how good, how understanding, how smart, how loving, how caring, how beautiful, how strong, how charismatic you are, you will still have problems to face. No matter how much you attempt to hedge the bets in your favor, you will have a problem that's a guarantee. They will be hard no matter what so it is useless to avoid them – face them and face them until something new comes up. It is an inescapable fact of the game of life that obstacles will occur. Don't get down on yourself. The Supreme Being does provide a way for all of us to make the problems in life more bearable and meaningful.

One way that the Supreme Being makes problems bearable is that you have the power of choice. Pick a life of purpose and face the accompanying problems that come along with a noble cause and gain something inspirational that means something; that gives you a reason to get up each day and face the world.

Mahatma Gandhi, Martin Luther King Jr., Nelson Mandela, Harriet Tubman, Rosa Parks and many, many, other men and women who chose a life that was meaningful are all heroes. They made a difference and faced unimaginable hardships and transformed the lives of us all in the problems they sought out to face and solve. [Humanity at its best.]

I'm not suggesting that you have to perform as they did to make a difference. Inside the simple act of choosing to make a difference, you may find that the "problems" you face aren't so difficult anymore. So take action. Get your education so you can get the job of your dreams. Learn to play the guitar. Pick up several different languages. Go skydiving. Challenge yourself and be fully engaged in your life. Become a Stand-Up Comedian. Take on becoming a world-class chef. Any of these things will be problematic, but it's pressing on past the hardships that make it all worthwhile. Problems you can have fun solving are key to living up to your full life's potential. You can choose to save as many people from suffering in the world as you can. That's what I'm striving for and my petty problems don't seem so significant anymore and I'm having fun doing it.

Wise Elder Tidbit:

God gives us difficulties so that we will always want to learn new things, to overcome them, and in doing so realize the potential of the power we possess thus experiencing the indisputable power of our brilliant creator.

> Mistakes are part of being human. Appreciate your mistakes for what they are; precious life lessons that can only be learned the hard way unless it's a fatal mistake, which at least others can learn from.
> – Al Franken

> Statistically – 100% of the shots you don't take, don't go in.
> – Wayne Gretzsky

[Curiosity Piece]

"Have you ever wondered why people love their pets so much?" Pets (animals) have set mental programming and will gravitate to a tolerant species that provides its comforts for living. They don't love you because they can't intellectually comprehend the uniquely human concept of unconditional acceptance/love of another being. "So why do we love our pets so much?" It's simply that we live our lives vicariously through our pets. The pets have basically a trouble free life with all of their amenities provided for them every day. We only wish we had it so good. It certainly feels good to provide a better less problematic life to another being. It gives us hope that our lives will be great too.

> Character cannot be developed in ease and quiet. Only through experience of trial and suffering can the soul be strengthened, vision cleared, ambition inspired, and success achieved.
> – Helen Keller

> Your living is determined not so much by what life brings you as by the attitude you bring to life; not so much by what happens to you as by the way your mind looks at what happens.
> – Lewis L. Dunnington

SOCIETY

> Please accept my resignation. I don't want to belong to any club that will accept me as a member.
> – *Groucho Marx*

Marasmus is a disease that killed infants in the early days of the United States' existence. Researchers found that no matter how great the care in the best of orphanages, if babies were denied human contact, holding and touching, the infants would eventually die. Nothing could save them but loving human contact. The power of touch is seen in this case very clearly. In orphanages with much less money and resources, babies lived and even thrived, as long as they were held and loved. This case is so significant because it shows us the degree to which all human beings need each other's physical presence and contact. We are all connected and require a connection through human interactions in order to live. No matter what possessions we have if we do not have socialization and contact with other humans, we are doomed. It wasn't a lack of proper nutrition and clean diapers that killed the babies; it was the loss of love through human contact. You could say that the babies appeared to die from losing the will to live in an unloving world.

"Let's go to the movies." "I can't wait to get to the basketball game…" "Sorry, got to go – it's time for my massage…"

"What is Society?"

Society fills an innate need for organisms to congregate together, en masse, for the general desire of companionship, fellowship, community, the sharing of ideas through language, for protection, sharing resources, and the sharing of intellect.

There are many Human societies throughout the world filled with a myriad of different cultures, religious beliefs, and ideas of how a functioning society can be. Society offers something that is most critical for the survival of human beings: Human contact. Human contact is absolutely essential to being human in this world. It does not take long for the human mind to slip into madness and incur a speedy end to its boring existence without it. The community involved in human contact creates the world of human beings.

> If you were all alone in the universe with no one to talk to, no one with which to share the beauty of the stars, to laugh with, to touch, what would be your purpose in life which gives your life meaning? This is harmony. We must discover the joy of each other, the joy of the challenge, the joy of growth.
> – *Mitsugi Saotome*

> We must rapidly shift from a "thing-oriented" society to a "person oriented" society. When machines and computers, profit motives, and property rights are considered more important than people, the giant triplets of racism, materialism, and militarism are incapable of being conquered.
> – *Martin Luther King, Jr.*

So, we as human beings need certain amounts of stimulation from each other to maintain a proper functional brain / computer program. It could also be offered that human beings love and desire to have children so much because we innately know that without propagation, societies would die out from boredom and humans as a species would too.

To sum it up, I'm glad to be a part of your society. Welcome to my family.

GOOD AND BAD

Case in Point:

There are people who love to participate in the fetish known as corpophagia (the use of fecal matter as a means to gain sexual gratification). This person eats feces (poop), and it gives him / her bliss. On the other hand, a person that is not into corpophagia would consider this practice as being indescribably deplorable. It is the very same act, but in one person's eyes, it is good – and in the other person's eyes it is bad.

"I wish you were never born." "What religion are you?" "How much money do you have?" "Have you ever been convicted of a crime?"

"What is Good and Bad?"

"Good" and "Bad" are mental interpretations and judgments of things and situations made by human beings. These interpretations/judgments can cause either disruptions (bad) or pleasure (good). We spend an enormous amount of our time reacting to things, situations, people, and the things that people say to us always interpreting what is good and bad about them. Perception is really the only precursor to what is good and bad to human beings. People instantly proceed to give meaning to whatever any situation is by determining that it is good or bad.

Remember: All of the following and preceding words are all lies.

There is no such thing as good or bad in reality Good and Bad actually do not exist.

> I believe that ignorance is the root of all evil. And that no one knows the truth.
> – Molly Ivins

> No man consciously chooses evil because it is evil; he only mistakes it for the happiness that he seeks.
> – *Mary Wollstonecraft Shelly*

Case in Point:

Deadly chemicals taken in very small doses (immunizations) can heal you and protect you from that disease. Conversely, prescription drugs used to heal and treat, if taken in high doses, can kill you.

Still More Examples:

- A thief may state that the only crime I committed was the crime of getting caught.
- A dictator could say that he had to kill millions of people for the greater good of the republic.
- Some people say that a male wearing his hair long is ugly.
- Other people may say that their day is not going well because it is raining outside.

Good and bad are perception-based only. What is one man's junk is another man's treasure it is all relative. What is happening when we evaluate anything is that our pre-existing life experience downloaded by our brain programs uses our past life as a judgment gage. It is our programming that determines what is good and what is bad. Nothing that exists in the world is good or bad. Brain computer programs vary and are distinct in every individual due to the differences present in the environment, economic holdings, life experiences with other humans, sex, age, self-awareness, intellect, educational level, and so on.

So, when a person states, "I am not saying that it is good or bad – I'm just stating that it is what it is – they are telling the truth.

> Nothing is good or bad but that our thinking makes it so.
> – *William Shakespeare*

When choosing between two evils, I always like to try the one I never tried before.
– *Mae West-Actress*

I just want to be good.
– *"X" (7 years old in trouble at school)*

GENIUS

> After all, being misunderstood is the fate of all true geniuses is it not?
> – Howard Stern (King of All Media) – Movie – Private Parts

> Genius may have its limitations, but stupidity is not thus handicapped.
> – Filbert Hubbard

… "She's so smart that she scored very high on the IQ test" … "He's dumb because he never completed high school"…

"What is Genius?"

Genius is the capacity of human beings to take a complicated concept and make it clear and simple to comprehend and the capability to pass on that clarity and comprehension to other human beings in a way that they too see it as simple and use it for the greater good.

To all of the people who scored high on the IQ test: Congratulations! You are a genius. Genius level in the IQ test indicates a person's capacity for acquiring knowledge. A person called a "genius" presents an extremely high capacity for learning and discovering new things. To all of the people who scored low in the "genius" level of the IQ test "Congratulations to you also!" because you are capable of discovering your genius as well as the next human being. Truly genius dwells in each and every one of us. All that is necessary is to be courageous enough to recognize and declare your particular expertise and pursue the life of your dreams. It is the selfishly arrogant shortsighted people who do not recognize that people who do not score at the genius level on tests are people who may still produce extraordinary results.

My personal genius lies in massage therapy, cooking vegetarian food that people love to eat, and philosophy, but I stink at math and spelling. I'm getting better at it (thank God for spell check).

Discover what you are innately suited for in this world and go for it. You may not score high on standardized tests, but you do have a higher purpose. So if you wish to live a life of peace, commit yourself to creating opportunities to foster your individual genius, and share it with the world. Whether you are the fastest ditch-digger known to man, a teller of the funniest jokes, a writer, inventor, artist, musician, humanitarian, floor scrubber, fighter, natural healer, golfer, or philosopher, be brave and give what talents you choose to focus on everything you've got. Follow your genius. The world will be a better place and you will become enlightened in the journey along the way.

> My philosophy is that not only are you responsible for your life, but doing the best at this moment puts you in the best place for the next moment.
> – *Oprah Winfrey*

DRUGS

... "I just really like getting high"... "I only drink socially"... "My life has been ruined because of my drug abuse"...

The author simply known as "X" is a reformed drug dealer. I was running with the wrong crowd and allowed myself to be seduced by all of the money, cars, and pretty girls available to a young man in the drug game (just like Darth Vader was seduced by the Evil Emperor in Star Wars). I was frustrated with my low paying job situation and it seemed to me like it was a victimless crime. My fellow thugs told me about all of the fringe benefits but they neglected to tell me about the shootings, stabbings, armed robberies by other thugs and dealers, beatings, relentless undercover police pursuit, betrayal by informants, and murders that came with the territory. I never really thought at the time that people actually died from the drug game; it seemed like I was doing addicts a favor getting them high and I was getting paid a lot of money.

One day I saw a young lady who had purchased drugs from me three months earlier and now she looked pregnant. I asked her how long she was pregnant and she said, "About six months." This was a twist I did not see coming I had sold drugs to a pregnant woman whom I did not know was pregnant and she did not tell me. I was outraged and told her to get into a drug rehab program and never come see me for drugs again. Now I began to see how terrible the drug game really was. I could see clearly the people dying from overdoses, families being destroyed by their own sons and daughters who would do or steal anything to get the next drug fix. I had to face the stark reality that I could be hurting innocent unborn babies who did not deserve to start their innocent little lives hooked on drugs. I had become in my mind a despicable monster and the fast women, gold necklaces, matching sweat suits, and designer sneakers quickly lost their luster. So after one very dramatic year in the drug game, I quit the business and six months later I was arrested for drug trafficking, convicted, and spent 2 years of my life in the mosquito infested, sun baked, unforgiving prison hell in the Great State of Mississippi. I'm very fortunate, many of my co-drug dealers died from lead poisoning (bullet wounds) or are serving life in prison with no possibility of parole. Makes you want to play the drug game for yourself aye boys and girls?

"What are Drugs?"

Drugs are chemicals from natural or man-made (synthetic) sources that provide a so-called "escape" for us from our brain-computer's programming. Drugs affect our brain and fool us into believing that we have escaped from the challenging circumstances of reality. Drugs also give us potential cures from ailments, have the ability to calm the mind, stimulate the mind, cause voluntary or involuntary physical harm, and oftentimes cause harmful alterations of our mental state. Drugs can cause a wide variety of effects, ranging from feelings /experiences of bliss, to horrifying hallucinations.

Drugs are in essence, a quick formative access to obtaining the illusion of winning at the game of life. Whether drugs are used to care for people with painful diseases or for recreation / fun drugs create the illusion of Peace. People utilize drugs to give them an immediate, false sense of peace and happiness. Unfortunately, over time, continued drug use will erase any possibility of personal peace through the mechanism of addiction (a preventable disease). Recreational drugs and alcohol affect the brain's computer programming, and over time, continuous use of these chemicals strips away much needed brain cells called neurons. We are born with all of the brain cells we will ever possess and our bodies do not have the ability to regenerate brain cells the way the body generates skin cells. Once a brain cell is destroyed, that's it game over for that cell. Loss of brain cells causes severe corruption of your programming that has developed over your lifetime. More often than not, these disruptions doom the individual drug user to a life of sheer survivalism; nothing else is possible. Your life is boxed in and over. A life all about survival is a sorrowful state of being the "living dead" appearing to be alive. There is nothing really going on past the survival program.

If you suffer from drug addiction, please seek help before it's to late. I have lost many good friends to drugs and their involvement with the sale of drugs. No matter how many times it takes for you go in and out of treatment, hang in there. Get well and my prayers are with you.

> I never believed in evil until a long time friend I know became a crack-head and he told me that smoking cocaine was better than sex. For once in my life I was scared to hope for a better world.
> – "X"

RELIGION

… "I'm Muslim"… "I'm Christian"… "I'm Jewish"… "I'm Hindu"… "I'm Buddhist"… "I'm an Atheist"…

> Men never do evil so completely and cheerfully as when they do it from religious conviction.
> – *Blaise Pascal*
>
> The quickest way for a man to get rich is to start his on religion.
> – *Unknown*

"What is Religion?"

Often all or some of the following description applies:

Religion is a chosen or forced way of life involving the use, or practice of prayers, fasting, meditation, rituals, cultural exchange, aestheticism, lectures, singing, chanting, donation, congregation, moral evaluation, atonement, the reading of selected texts (both ancient and modern), myths, allegories, and spiritual practices/actions – all or part of these above actions done solely for fear of persecution, joy, or respect of a higher power or being.

Religion includes the belief of a higher power, and/or authoritative hierarchal humans, or sometimes non-human deities/entities. It includes the hopes of being transformed to a higher state of grace in this life or the next, or both. Religion comes in many forms, most claiming to be the one, the only, and the true way to spiritual salvation. Religion involves seeking something meaningful within the existence of life. Usually religions influence their congregations and followers in every tangible move in life, from politics to all social relationship exchanges. Translations of texts or writings from the past by people espousing a particular religious focus play key roles in revealing hard-line truths about what it means to be a human in the service of God.

Case in Point:

Move the newborn French baby again – now it is a Muslim-born baby, and it is put into a Christian family. The baby will be a Christian child because environment has such a strong religious influence on humans. The human *need* to be part of a social group and to be accepted strongly directs what religious beliefs we chose to claim mental ownership of and in doing so shapes the entire way we react to people throughout our lives. To human beings acceptance equals love.

Religion really only needs to have two measurable principles regardless of denomination. For example it is common to most religions to do the following:

1. Love, honor, and respect the Creator (higher power).
2. Treat other human beings the way you wish to be treated, in all interactions, great or small. (Nearly all of what humans consider honorable and decent rings true of these 2 simple principles.)

Granted, you can follow those two principles without being part of an official organized religion. Nevertheless, if you enjoy the security and acceptance of your chosen religious group, and it helps you to create peace for yourself and others, by all means continue to be a part of your religion.

Beware! If your religion promotes intolerance of other people because of differing personal or religious beliefs from other religious denominations, refuses to let you question its practices and doctrines, or takes away the bulk of your personal finances and quality time. You may want to entertain other religious options available to you in your transition towards peace and salvation.

I know for a fact that God reveals himself/herself/itself in all peaceful religions even though they vary greatly in outward appearance and function. If this were not a fact, there would never be one moment's peace between most of the countries in the world with the staggering number of religious sects circumventing the globe. So if other religions were as ungodly as we think they are, nuclear winter would be upon us right now. "X" couldn't possibly write this book with a frozen backside and no electricity. Historically great humanitarian works of kindness have manifested from all of the worlds great religions.

> God loves all people and you can also if you choose.
> – "X"

> And when you call to prayer they make it a mockery and a joke; this is because they are people who do not understand.
> – The Koran

> "Be strong and of good courage, fear not, nor be afraid… for the Lord thy God, he is that doth go with thee; he will not fail thee, nor forsake thee."
> – The Holy Bible

> As the air is everywhere, flowing around a pot and filling it, so God is everywhere, filling all things and flowing through them forever.
> – Ashtavakra Gita 1:18 – 20 Hindu Texts

> The mind, the Buddha, living creatures- these are not three different things.
> – Avatamasaka Sutra

> Qua-Omsa-Lajuwann [translation] All praises unto the light.
> – Authors of - The Coming of Tan - Friend Riley Martin and Tan (the Extraterrestrial) Biaviian Alien Religion

EDUCATION

Congratulations on having graduated high school, college, post-college, and trade/vocational certification program!

"What's next?"

"What is Education?"

Education is mental interaction with all incoming data within your sphere of awareness in order to acquire knowledge and/or skills applicable to living life. You receive, transfer, modify, and comprehend data with your computer brain and add it to your existing programming. Education is usually pursued to better one's life and/or the lives of others.

Education is a transformational process. Modern day education differs greatly from the education of the past, but rest assured that education has always been around. Since the days of the caveman Mankind has been bettering himself/herself for survival and enjoyment. Education obviously works because man as a species is still around.

Education varies from person to person, community to community, country to country, continent to continent, endlessly transforming, updating, refining, and improving throughout recorded time and history.

Much like Religion, education is also to a great extent influenced by its environment, location, government, scale in time, and further motivated by the need for human acceptance. The more educated a person is the more likely he/she is to be admired, respected, and highly valued by family members, peers, and usually included in frequent social activities.

Case in Point:

In America some corporations may apply for upwards of fifty patents for new ideas in one day. But in some other countries, they may apply for twenty patents for ideas over a twenty-year period. In other words: The environment of one country reinforces the need for new and innovative ideas while other countries for whatever reasons do not promote progressive thinking.

Educating oneself is the only way to obtain self-awareness and true self-expression. Many governments and / or communities recognize this and create strict measures of what will be presented to the masses in order to gain and maintain control of the populace. It is considered easier to ride a docile horse than a bucking bronco. It is easier to function in the way of the Queen bee of a collective hive where every member thinks in the same manner and performs his / her jobs without question or rebellion.

If you are fortunate enough to live in a society where you can educate yourself free of constraints, please do so and enhance the purpose you were born to fulfill. Let the meaning of your life shine through your education and influence your educational choices. Your idea of education may not include a four-year college degree, or even any certifications, but remain open and diligent. If your desire is to be fully self-aware and self-expressed, pursue the completion of this noble cause with dedication and diligence. Allow the genius that is part of your life to blossom into the world.

> Oftentimes the difference between life and death, love and hate, war and peace, freedom and oppression, is a BOOK.
> – "X"

POLITICS

... "Ask not what your country can do for you – ask what you can do for your country"... "Friends, Romans, and Countrymen"...

> In my country we go to prison first and then we become president.
> – *Nelson Mandela*

"What is Politics?"

Politics, by many, is considered to be governmental involvement in the rules, regulations, foreign and domestic policies, and taxation of citizens for the greater good of the entire populace.

> Politics is war without bloodshed while war is politics with bloodshed.
> – *Mao Tse-Tung*

This is correct, but it is a very limited view in the assessment of what politics really portray. Politics not only involves governmental interaction with people, but also encompasses all interactions within the total populace. This includes friends, family, strangers, and the rest of the world of people; all carry the weight of politics.

Case in Point:

Having dinner with your boss and having dinner with your best friend are situations that are handled very differently.

"Why?" Because the social expectations are different the tone you take with your best friend may be jovial and lighthearted:

"Hey Best Friend? What do you call a bull with no legs? – Ground beef!!!"

Whereas the tone with your boss is more serious and oriented primarily towards the conduction of business:

"Say Boss, who do I have to kiss in the office to get a raise around here?" Well, maybe a little more serious than that.

Nearly every communicative interaction we have with other human beings is a mental juggling act of what personal politics we have to use to get what we want or need from other individuals. We literally coerce our way through life. "Do you interpret this coercion as a good or bad thing?" Remember good and bad are only your personal translations of life's situations.

Going back to the discussion of government and its role in life there is a very old cliché: "Absolute power corrupts absolutely." Oftentimes this can become a grim reality involving even the most democratic of world governments.

Even in ancient Roman history some of the most tyrannical of its emperors started out as great humanitarians, concerned with human welfare. Eventually after some period of time in power, they created and acted upon some of the greatest atrocities ever recorded in human history. "Why?"

All of these abuses of power can be traced back to our "survival program" that can run our lives completely if not kept in check. The survival program drives all creatures to live at the cost and expense of other creatures' well being if they think it is necessary. If the kindest people around are not fortunate enough to become educated and enlightened as to the oneness of the nature of life and understand what mechanisms drive and fuel their desires, they can in time be swayed to the dark side of their survival program. Acquiring massive amounts of power will more often than not kick the survival program into overdrive, and the human being will lose touch with reality. He will react to perceived and implied threats to his power in the same manner as he would react to a real physical threat. His programming tells him that these implied mental thoughts rambling around in his head represents very real intimidating threats.

Without the boundaries of self-awareness and the oneness around us, it is inevitable that the outcome of abundant power is to veer off the path of Peace. Survival programming can and does make many that you love and care about the monsters in your/our future. Programming can fool you into believing that even the people closest to you are demons in disguise. You must volunteer to intervene and share insightful information and trust that sharing will make a difference. It is only in the sharing of political information that we as individuals can deter horrible offenses from occurring in the future. Such is the true power of politics.

> There is a basic law that "like attracts like". Negative thinking definitely attracts negative results. Conversely, if a person habitually thinks optimistically and hopefully, his positive thinking sets in motion creative forces – and success, instead of eluding him, flows to him.
> – *Norman Vincent Peale*

> "Why are you unhappy?" It's because 99% of everything you do, and say, and think, is for yourself.
> – *Wei Wu Wei (Terence Gray)*

MONEY

We like it! We love it! We need more of it! ... "Money makes the world go round"...

> If you really want something in life, you have to work for it – now quiet they're about to announce the lottery numbers!
> – Homer Simpson - TV Cartoon Personality - The Simpson's

"What is Money?"

Money is an agreed upon and established form of currency used to obtain goods and services, as opposed to bartering (trading). Money was developed to make resources and labor more liquid, tradable, and transferable. Precious metals/jewels such as gold, silver, and diamonds establish the value of certified legal tender. The exchange of paper notes, and/or coinage (legal tender) to speed up and regulate the process of financial interactions is currency in use.

It is often said that money is the root of all-evil. If only that were true, we could burn all the money in existence and cause instantaneous world peace.

> He who will not economize will have to agonize.
> – Confucius

For many of us, money seems to be the root of our problems in life. This concept is ingrained in us from childhood the instant we comprehend that you have to have money to get the things you want. Humans consider that a lack of sufficient money is the cause of our perceived difficulties. In fact, the presence or absence of amounts of money in our bank accounts is never the problem. Pursuing and spending money is simply a mask covering our fears and insecurities we have inside of us. To be sure, we all look at not having any money as a very real problem but is that the whole of it?

> If you have no money, be polite.
> – *Danish Proverb*

Case in Point:

People who have a lot of money hoard it to maintain their personal illusions of power. Some rich people who believe they rule other peoples' lives are in fact slave to their own survival programming. This is because having money is all an illusion. You can possess stacks of money or gold bullion, and what you have is stacks of paper and blocks of metal. You do not have money. Monetary materials only function as valuable simply because of human agreements about monies applicable worth. People have to agree to the power of money in order for money to have power at all. So people with lots of money instinctively exploit people with less money, in order to further their "survival programming" in the hopes of living lives of great comfort without fears.

The rich suffer as much as the poor by subconsciously seeking to oppress instead of spreading the wealth because they falsely believe in the vision that they don't have enough money to share with the less fortunate because they might lose their control over poor people frightens them. So you see, whether you have money or not, the experience is always one of suffering.

People *without* money use this as an excuse to wallow in self-loathing, self-pity, and unwarranted and pointless resentment of others with more material goods than themselves. This thought process allows selfish justification of the individuals' lack of performance in living a happy life because false judgments and a poor minded attitude causes the person to fail to utilize his/her own genius to acquire more resources, and the talking in the head worrying blocks him/her from achieving greater self-awareness. Facing the challenges head-on is the only way to enlightenment, inner / outer peace, and monetary wealth. Otherwise you create your world as "I have nothing so I am nothing." Money is just a tool, the same as a hammer is a tool to a carpenter, or a spatula to a cook. Money is not an all-powerful source of peace and happiness, or a present evil.

Case in Point:

Try this exercise: Be honest with yourself and others close to you about your present financial status. If you cannot afford something at a particular time, be honest and forthcoming about this. This doesn't mean that you stop enjoying your life; it just means you are being straight about your current financial situation. Start developing a greater self-awareness and control over your experience with your finances. Out-of-control spending to keep up (false) appearances of wealth to other people is a complete waste of precious energy and time. Frankly, thinking in this way borders on madness. Start giving money to charities of your choice. Only generosity creates generosity, and it is ok to expect generosity in return. Focus on prosperity not debt all the time this will channel your energy in the right direction to create the wealth you desire.

Money is not the problem; you are the problem. The way in which you view money is the actual "problem" that you experience around money; unfortunately many times rich and famous people kill themselves either purposely or subconsciously because their huge amounts of money and adulation fail to produce the magical results of happiness, peace, and purpose they expected to encounter with the trappings of fame (after all this is what most people believe that riches and fame are the proverbial magic wand). This causes severe depression and disenfranchisement with their lives and life itself becomes tedious and meaningless to them.

Let me share with you something about my personal life about money. I experience struggle around money as much as anyone, so I began to ponder my dilemma. I am an intelligent human being, "So why does money worry me to such a painful extent?" I have a roof over my head, a car, and a refrigerator full of food, "So why does money bother me so much?" Then it came to me – money wasn't the problem. The problem exists in my programming. I was not educated about money and how it works in my early childhood years (Teach Kids about MONEY early on to secure it in their programming). My family and friends were not helpful in regards to teaching me about how to make money work for me. So money occurred for me as – I work for money, money doesn't work for me.

Money is just an agreement amongst people and people are the resource. Empowered with this fact I know without a shadow of a doubt that I am not alone in the world and never again would I live in this world solely believing that I am by myself when it comes to making income. I was caught up in the mental trap of working for money, rather than the other way around. I would worry about my ability to handle money properly, rather than to actually get into action and handle my money. I just worried endlessly about my innate "ability" to handle it, so I never got anywhere. Also I noticed that my survival programming went into overdrive because of the fear of financial ruin I gave power too.

Case in Point:

I felt deep down that I would become completely penniless and be at the mercy of strangers in a world where strangers care nothing about what happens to me. Looking at the homeless people on the streets of our inner cities, I was frightened that at any moment that could be me begging on the street. It was this sobering experience of this particular fear/uncertainty about me and not money that blocked me from having the tool of abundant money for use in causing peace in my life and in the world. I promise you it was not easy to really sit down and think about why I was so fearful about money. It was akin to pulling teeth but now my life is so much richer because I have gained control over my emotions about finances in this regard. I stopped myself from worrying about money and it freed my mind and energy so that I could create the wealth I desired.

The way you treat your money is the same way you treat the people in your intimate relationships. If you look first at your relationships to compare you will not see the correlation, but if you look at the money relationship itself without focusing on your personal relationships you will see how you are in your intimate relationships.

Case in Point:

Honestly – "How many people do you know will completely divorce all of their money before they will divorce their mates?" Include yourself and I mean every penny you've got.

Personally I would take my mate's money, and my money and make a run for the hills! We do love our money. This is why Kidnappers don't ask for all of your money because if they did, they would get strong arms and shoulders digging ditches and declare bankruptcy because of lack of wages received. It really doesn't say much about our faith in the creator but after all we are only human.

Here is another thing about our relationship to money. If you are stingy and hog money, you will be stingy in the bedroom with your mate. If you are frightened about losing money, you will be frightened insecure and untrusting in relationships. If you are generous with money, you will be giving in the intimacy department. Money is really our closest intimate relationship – only it's with dead presidents instead of living people. So, find your relationship to money and see what inhibits you from abundance and happiness. Free yourself from past fears and money will become present for you in surprising and powerful ways. My big fear was about losing money and not having enough so to gain power over that fear I gave away tons of money to charities and friends. This was a very hard thing because I was scared about my future, but I persisted. Then I began to receive higher paying jobs and working fewer hours for more pay and the fear I had about money begin to lose its grip on me. I can't describe to you how liberating it is to battle through that fear and not have it run my life anymore; it's like I have a new set of lungs. I transformed the rules of the money game that I played and the universe did the rest. Ladies I'm very generous with money so do the math.

> Most people work just hard enough not to get fired and get paid just enough not to quit.
> – *George Carlin*

> If a rich man is proud of his wealth, he should not be praised until it is known how he employs it.
> – *Socrates*

Money does not make a person kind, caring, and loving; Money does not and never will function to make you more powerful, problem-free, and better than the next human being.

- Realize that you have enough money for what you need right now.
- Be generous with money, time, and resources and the world will generate and be generous back to you.
- Ally yourself with wealthy influential people. If you don't know at least five people you can borrow $1,000 from (other than family) you're running with the wrong crowd and limiting the borders of your world. Even the most thuggish of Rap Stars (musical rhyming artists) are friends with wealthy businessmen with legitimate businesses.
- You quickly need to expand your world by attending social functions where you can make friends with

influential people, not to scheme or use them, but to share, listen, and learn from a humble student's point of view. In the meantime, don't chuck away your current family and friends because they still love and need you, and in your pursuit to expand your social boundaries keep them close because all you are doing is adding other friends into the mix. Do this and you will eventually be able to pass on your good fortune and great friends to those you really care about.

Admire others success and learn from them.
– Chinese Proverb

All the gold in the world cannot buy a dying man one more breath – so what does that make today worth?
– Og Mandino

Wise Elder Tidbit:

One day a man walked up to me on the street and begged for some change (coins of money). I told the man I would give him twenty dollars to buy a yard rake and for him to meet me at my home the following morning. The man arrived the next day and raked the leaves, and I said, "If you want a steady job take this money I'm giving you for raking the leaves and by a lawn mower and I will pay you a fair wage." The man purchased a nice push lawn mower and I told him he could check with the neighbors as well for yard work and that I would put in a good word for him. Eventually the homeless man became a successful lawn care professional and now lives a dignified taxpaying life, not being a burden to himself or anyone else. If you are blessed with money never despair over your good fortune. It is yours to do with it as you wish, but giving money alone is not enough. Helping someone to help himself is the greatest thing you can do for your fellow man.

RACE

Nigger, kike, red-man, slant-eye, towel-head, spic, honkey, camel jockey, fag, dike, greaser... Words people call each other. Not so pretty when you see it in writing.

"What is Race?"

Race is a scientific classification, categorizing human beings according to their physical similarities. Race is a point of reference for a particular group of people with a certain amount of similar physical characteristics mostly due to the color of their skin.

The illusion of race is that human beings are their differences. There is an illusion perpetrated that we are somehow separate because the color of our skin varies.

Case in Point:

The scientific, biological facts are that we as human beings are all one species (Homo sapiens), generated from one common source of biogenetic origin. Proof of this fact is evident and apparent inside the coding of human mitochondria DNA. It is identical indicating that we all have the same common origin. [The first Eve if you will.] Also, skin color around which people so closely relate to as a distinct difference in humans, has been scientifically proven to be only a matter of different shades of brown. So, the whitest Caucasian, the yellowiest Asian, the blackest Negro, the reddest Native American, and the brownest Hispanic, are all part of the human continuum of skin shading in the governing color spectrum of brown.

If skin shading were actually an indication of a species difference, then the so-called "cross-breeding" between different colors of humans, would be impossible. Crossbreeding between different species is virtually a physical impossibility. Generally no offspring are possible and even if an offspring were possible, the result would be a sterile organism unable to reproduce itself. We are all aware that human beings can produce fertile offspring, regardless of differences in the color of their parents. In this way, the Supreme Being has ensured that only living beings meant to reproduce can reproduce over and over again naturally.

Case in Point:

Some people have taken it upon themselves to interbreed lions and tigers (ligers). Even though these two animals seem to have everything important in common, they are a different biological species. As such, any Ligers produced are 100% sterile. There is a very low occurrence of Ligers being born at all because attempts to breed two Ligers have been completely unsuccessful. Ligers are huge in physical size and they are the biggest cats on earth, but they can't make babies.

Human Beings, regardless of color, have no problems whatsoever reproducing. The problems we have gravitated around are race relations. The relationships between races of human beings cause countless problematic issues here on planet earth. People in power in society have created race as a reason to subdue people for their own perverse reasons. Race classification is a form of mental separation and control. Factors such as war, history of slavery and oppression, economic inequality, lack of education, limited self-awareness, forced ignorance, along with the continual perpetration of stereotypes are the actual culprits and barriers to harmonious relations between the so called races.

In reality, there are only Human Beings; Race is all an illusion.

> Almost always, the creative dedicated minority has made the world better.
> – Dr. Martin Luther King, Jr.

> I'm for human liberation, the liberation of all people, not just black people, or female or gay people.
> – Richard Pryor

RACE

He who allows oppression shares the crime.
– *Erasmus Darwin*

If there is no justice, there is no peace.
– *Bahya ben Asher*

Famous Last Word:

Freedom!!!
– *William Wallace – Scottish Patriot*

To see humanity with colorblind eyes awakens ancient wisdom.
– *"X"*

POWER

Case in Point:

If the greatest dictators of the world spouted foul rhetoric on deaf ears, "How many millions of people would still be alive?" The dictator himself did not possess the power; he simply persuaded the people to follow his will collectively and the power to commit mass murder was established. Power always has to be given. What occurs in dictatorships on a large scale also happens on a small (yet not insignificant) scale in our everyday lives. "How often do we go to jobs we hate, work with people we dislike, put up with insufficient pay, and live with rules we don't agree with?" " Who is giving the power to whom in that situation? Can the power be regained if you will it?" Yes it can.

… "I've got the power!"… "Money is power"… "You have no power over me"…

"What is Power?"

Power is an occurrence that exists when one organism can persuade another organism that it must move in the direction of the persuasive organisms' will to fulfill the personal, or collective agenda of the organism doing the persuading. Power in the experience of human beings generally means that if you get the biggest guns, the most money, and/or the strongest political backing, than you can command people to do nearly anything that you desire. Most people will in fact follow through with commands to do whatever you desire if you prove your position as a perceived social authority figure.

POWER

> Nearly all men can stand adversity, but if you want to test a man's character, give him power.
> – *Abraham Lincoln*

All of the power that any one person or group of people has is purely given to them. Even under the most extreme of circumstances, you can be physically abducted and / or threatened with death, but a response to someone else's commands is a given thing. In other words, power cannot exist in a vacuum. You must be willing to comply with personal physical action for power to be created. Force is force, not power. Real power is given and cannot be taken.

Examine your life and see where you are powerless, because powerless cannot exist because you and only you possess your freedom of choice.

Areas such as employment / occupation / career, money, and relationships are common areas where we feel powerless in tense situations. Confront these negative feelings in thought, talk to someone you can trust, and take action to regain the power you already possess. Quit the horrible job, find another job, or find a way to make the job you hate better. Sure there is the potential that you will encounter problems, but no matter what you will always have to encounter problems. Dare yourself to be happy.

The power to create a beautiful life is yours. Use it!!!

> Where justice is denied, where poverty is enforced, where ignorance prevails, and where any one class is made to feel that society is an organized conspiracy to oppress, rob and degrade them, neither persons nor property will be safe.
> – *Frederick Douglass*

There will be no end to troubles of states, or of humanity itself, till philosophers become kings in this world, or till those we now call kings and rulers really and truly become philosophers, and political power and philosophy thus come into the same hands.
— *Plato*

The wave of the future is not the conquest of the world by a single dogmatic creed but the liberation of the diverse energies of free nations and free men.
— *John F. Kennedy*

Most people have no idea of the giant capacity we can immediately command when we focus all of our resources on mastering a single area of our lives.
— *Anthony Robbins*

INVENTION

> First say to yourself what you would be; and then do what you have to do.
> – *Epictetus*

… "You can become rich with this idea and invention"…
"I thought of that first – it's my invention!"…

"What is Invention?"

Invention is the unique ability of human beings to create tools, thoughts, ideas, and theoretical possibilities that heretofore never existed. Invention also includes improving upon inventions already created.

"Necessity is the mother of invention." Humans' ability to invent things that better and further the human living condition is nothing short of miraculous.

Let me ask you this question:

"Are you an inventor?"

If yes, "What have you invented?" If you are one of those brilliant inventors who have invented something of real use to the world, something that improves peoples' lives, then I applaud you wholeheartedly. If your answer to the question was no, then you have formed the wrong answer. Because you are one of the greatest inventors in the world – you invent yourself and your life anew each day, each moment.

Case in Point:

When you go to your job, does your job invent itself or do you invent your job every time you perform it? The job cannot exist without your creating it. Someone else may have offered you the set of tasks and rules that define the job outwardly, but no one creates your job the way you do and no one else will ever do your job the way you do, ever. You are a unique occurrence, a fantastic anomaly, and a brilliant star. Also the fact of the matter is you invent your very life every day. Whether you consider your life good or bad, you are the source that invents that good or bad life every moment of your life. You invent your style, your attitude, your point of view, and the direction in which you travel and those who are famous, who are rich, who are successful, created themselves so. You make you!

If you don't particularly care for the life you've created, invent a different one. Since the rules governing life are made up anyway, make up rules that create the life you desire. Invent a different set of rules and play the game full out. Every Human game has rules by human design, and we alone have the distinct capacity for changing the rules of life at will. Otherwise, there would never be freedom of choice because without freedom of choice, there would be no winners and losers – no self-made millionaires and billionaires. A billionaire is simply a human being who created him or herself to be such. Before Bill Gates hit it big with computers, he was on the streets of New York selling penny stocks in a company known as Microsoft. They made their own rules, played by them, and in the process created vast wealth. If they fail, they simply reinvent themselves. Witness the life of Donald Trump who lost billions and made it all back again. They are humans just like you and me.

Reinvention starts at the exact moment that a human being activates the most powerful computer in the universe – his / her very own Human brain. When we intervene and alter our

INVENTION

programming we accomplish the goals that we have created as urgent to achieve. We obtain these goals by utilizing verbal and physical communication combined with action, upon action, upon action, upon action, until the goal is reached. Invent a new you anytime. You are a master inventor my friend. Just trust in yourself and the universe will follow and make a way where there were only walls before.

> I never perfected an invention that I did not think about in terms of the service it might give others. I find out what the world needs, then I proceed to invent.
> – *Thomas Edison*

WAR

> There was never a good war or a bad peace.
> – Benjamin Franklin

… "They have weapons of mass destruction"… "They are a threat to our civilization/society/way of life"… "They have terrorized us for the last time"… "Retaliate!!!"… "Exterminate!!!"

"What is War?"

War is an openly hostile act of aggression by one or more organisms against another. War is waged for the sole purpose of acquiring a dominant position in which to dictate one or more of the following; terms for a satisfactory end to a hostile conflict, division or sole ownership of valuable resources (i.e. oil, plutonium, precious metals, human labor, sex, etc.) or to completely destroy the unfortunate loser usually by any means necessary.

> Can anything be stupider than a man has the right to kill me because he lives on the other side of the river and his ruler has a quarrel with mine, though I have not quarreled with him?
> – Blaise Pascal

> I know war as few other men now living know it, and nothing to me is more revolting. I have long advocated its complete abolition, as its very destructiveness on both friend and foe has rendered it useless as a method of settling international disputes.
> – General Douglas Macarthur

> You cannot trample upon people who are innocent and not expect retaliation.
> – Sylvester Stallone

Human beings have waged war on each other, (helpless animals not excluded), prior to the beginning of recorded history. Usually throughout recorded history the object of war has been for one group to plunder treasure from another, take over or annex territory, convert people to another religion, press humans into slavery, or to steal, destroy, or incorporate the defeated peoples' culture and valuables in any way the victors deem fit.

Thus, everyone's ancestors have more than likely at one time or another in history been enslaved or oppressed by their fellow man perhaps even converted or slain in the name of their enemies religious beliefs.

There is an old saying, "steal a little – and you are a thief, steal a lot – and you become a king." This statement rings loud and clear through the ages and into the present day.

Case in Point:

Because of a pervasive lack of self-awareness among human beings, the survival program still controls most people on the planet, including our modern day governments. Thus, the invention of nuclear bombs and other weapons of mass destruction were inevitable because governments put the bulk of its money, genius, and resources into mastering weapons of mass destruction. If weapons of mass destruction ceased to exist right now, the survival programming would go into overdrive and the resulting slaughter of the innocents would pale in comparison to anything the world has witnessed thus far.

Our collective goal should be, must be, to enlighten ourselves and bring it to the world as intelligently, peacefully, and as quickly possible. Truly the only way that we can ever stop any future war is to expand our conversations about peace to include action other than just reading the papers and being apathetically disgusted.

> I think now, looking back, we did not fight the enemy, we fought ourselves. The enemy was in us. The war is over for me now, but it will always be there, the rest of my days.
> – *Movie Platoon - Character Chris Taylor on the Vietnam War*

Really the greatest war is not with the enemies around us. The real war is with the enemy inside ourselves – the survival program itself. Our hyperactive survival programming blinds us with fears that make the decisions of our lives. Wrong education or the lack of education about the survival program and its effect on human nature fearfully blinds us to what really removes the peaceful choices in life that would be there for our perusal into politically solvable conflicts.

We create internal vulnerability, and in fact, live our lives as if internal vulnerability doesn't exist. We live like we are not programmed creatures and that is exactly what we are. We have to upgrade our thinking to upgrade the world we live in or primitive programming could make us all extinct and we definitely do not want that.

Blindness to our limitless potential is the tool the tyrants of the world willingly exploit and oftentimes convince others to dictate how life and death in our world will be rationed. Until we awaken ourselves to the reality of our power to go beyond our animalistic survival programming, the tyrants of the world will flourish and wars will continue; this is a startling certainty. Pass peace on to the next person who may be the person who changes the world for the better.

> You're not to be so blind with your patriotism that you can't face reality, wrong is wrong, no matter who does it or says it.
> – *Malcolm X*

CHILDREN

... "Sugar and spice and everything nice"... "Snips and snails and puppy dogs' tails"...

> We were born to succeed not to fail.
> – Henry David Thoreau

"What are Children?"

Children are newly created human beings, grown inside the abdominal cavity and uterus of a human female using genetic material (DNA) from both male and female human beings. The genetic materials, when combined inside the female womb, metamorphose to create another distinct human being in the form of a cute little baby.

> The first half of our lives is ruined by our parents, and the second half by our children.
> – Clarence Darrow

Children are the living embodiment of the future of humanity. We love children dearly, and it is a privilege and a gift to have children in our lives. Human beings in their quest for community and connection with one another are social beings and revel in the opportunity to be immortalized through the survival of our species by creating children. A great deal of the interaction with children is the process of raising them to be happy functional human beings. The raising process (interactive programming) requires a parent, preferably both parents, or a guardian or guardians, to provide food and water, love, and data for the child until the child can sufficiently provide those things for himself / herself.

Case in Point:

Raising children is difficult at best, and the raisers of children honestly do the best they can. "So how is it that children who come from the best of life situations turn out the worst?" "What is the magic formula and why is it that children who suffer the most horrible of life circumstances turn out so well?" These two extremes illustrate clearly that each human child, as with each human adult, is entirely unique, "So why the discrepancy in the outcomes?"

The wealthy family raising their child set very few boundaries and provide little access to the data necessary for the child to become self-aware and evolved mentally. On the other hand, the poor family has little access to material goods, but provide the access for their child to be self-aware and responsive to boundaries, held to high moral standards, and instill the assumption that he is personally responsible for his success in life. The development of integrity, self-awareness, self-expression, responsibility, and the opportunity to make a difference causes the poor child to become a person of value and contribution. I must also point out that this is not always the case. Poor kids often can be just as rotten and disrespectful to their fellow men and women without proper boundaries enforced.

> Where did we ever get the crazy idea that in order to make children do better, first we have to make them feel worse? Think of the last time you felt humiliated or treated unfairly. Did you feel like cooperating or doing better?
> – Jane Nelson

Children require identifiable boundaries to understand their purpose in life. An identifiable boundary is something that indicates a fair and just limit. Children, just like adults who have not been educated in self-awareness, live completely at the mercy of their survival program lacking the cognitive intelligence to filter out true threats to their well-being. The survival programming in a child respects little else besides force, and lack of force. And as lovely and cute as children are physically and spiritually, if adult human beings do not educate them from a reasonable dominant standpoint, the children will not develop suitable structural boundaries thus becoming a problem child and maybe a destructive adult.

> Human beings are the only creatures that allow their children to come back home.
> – Bill Cosby

> Making the decision to have a child – it's momentous. It is to decide forever to have your heart go walking outside your body.
> – Elizabeth Stone

> You know your children are growing up when they start asking questions that have answers.
> – John J. Plomp

> All children are artists. The problem is how to remain an artist once he grows up.
> – Pablo Picasso

> Don't limit a child to your own learning, for he was born in another time.
> – Rabbinical Saying

A lack of education coupled with a lack of proper boundary setting breeds resentment, frustration, and heated rebellion in children. Children respond to a lack of structure by seeing just how much further they can go without repercussions and each time they are allowed to emotionally roam unfettered, they build programming which says to them that there are no boundaries in the world. This warped view of the world sets children up for failure, self-destruction and / or the destruction of others.
So maintain firm but fair boundaries or FAMILY policy. Post it on the walls if you have to and provide education about self-awareness throughout childhood; it will better your chances of having well rounded, loving, intelligent, and respectful children.

That is if you do not have to constantly pick them up off the floor at the shopping mall when they can't have what they want. "Don't you hate when that happens?"

We must become more responsible parents for our children's sake. Do you know if you yell, belittle, threaten, beat, or ignore your children more than you sensibly talk to them 90% of the time, you are not raising your kids. Sure you feed and clothe them but what is raising your kids is the limited protocol governing your survival program. The three objectives governing your raising the kids are fear, unjust domination, and your personal comfort. Try doing the opposite of the survival protocol and have faith in God that compassion, understanding, and love will serve as the best taskmasters of your children's fate. Believe it or not, your children are your greatest investment for a comfortable, well-loved life in the future.

Case In Point:

My beautiful mother worked hard all of her life from picking cotton with her family as a little girl in Mississippi to working as a seamstress in a factory for nearly thirty years. One night she felt a sharp pain in her lower back and legs that roused her from a sound sleep and she needed to use the rest room. Mama finished using the rest room but she could not stand up; she was paralyzed from the waist down. Luckily she had a roommate that helped her to her bed and called 911 for an ambulance to pick her up. To make a long story short, severe arthritis of the spine (scientific name Spinal Stenosis) had squeezed her spinal cord so tight it paralyzed her from the waist down. Mother suffered through many months of trials and tribulations to learn how to walk again and her employer that she had worked for 28 years gave her a watch, laid her off her job, and cancelled her gravely needed health insurance. In America, that can be a death sentence.

If not for her having raised two little mischievous kids my sister and I, she would have been left for dead by the greedy government that took 2 years to qualify her for Medicare health insurance so that she could get the back surgery she needed 2 years earlier and landlords, and assisted living homes for the elderly don't take hardship stories for payment. Mom struggled as a single parent and the investment and love that she put into raising her two kids proved to be her salvation from poverty or worse. It brings tears to my eyes re-living it right now. I truly love my dear sweet mother and I'm not ashamed to say I would be nothing without her making a courageous stand for my life. Mother was there for me through the tough times – including prison, heartbreaks, and condemnation by people who felt it was their duty not to give me a second chance. I love you Mom, now and forever, and it is this quality of love by parent and child that can heal the planet.

I make a challenge to all of the parents in the world to stop letting TELEVISION, RADIO, and the INTERNET be the parents of our children. I know it keeps them quiet but it conditions them to see Media as the source of all truth and if you really think about this you can rationalize that indeed this estranged behavior is extremely dangerous in this day and age. Stand-up for the challenge because if you live long enough the parenting of your child will come full circle – guaranteed.

> Once I finish kindergarten, I'm going to find me a wife.
> – Tom Age 5

Native-American Parable:

One day a Father (without knowledge of the oneness of life) asked his Little Boy to take his Grandfather deep into the woods far from home so that he would no longer be a burden to him. The Little Boy being obedient reluctantly began to do as his father commanded even though he loved the elderly man very much. "Before you go son take this blanket with you and leave it with your Grandfather." The little boy grabbed the blanket and left with his grandfather into the woods. Many hours later, the Little Boy returned home with the blanket folded up in his hands. "Damn boy! I told you to leave that blanket with the old man! Why didn't you do what I said?" The Little Boy bravely replied, "I left Grandpa half of the blanket." "Why on earth did you do that?" his Father exclaimed. "Because I'm saving this half for you when you get old Papa." The Father grabbed his son by the hand and said, "Come on son lets go get Grandpa," and they all lived happily ever after. Meantime the Little Boy grew up to become a wise and powerful chief, husband, father, and loyal caretaker to his elderly Father.

The moral of the story is – be good to the kids. You never know when you might need a kidney or something.

> How sharper than a serpent's tooth it is to have a thankless child.
> –*William Shakespeare – from King Lear*

> Savor the smiles and laughter of your children – there is nothing more important.
> – *Gary W. Fenchuk*

MUSIC

... "I want to rock and roll all night"... "I am the best rapper alive"... "I can't live without music"...

> My music will go on forever. Maybe it's a fool say that, but when me know facts me can say facts. My music will go on forever.
> – Bob Marley

"What is Music?"

Music is noise organized by humans in ways that are pleasing and cater to their particular interest. Music is strategically designed and composed to generate and cause a desired emotional and oftentimes physical response. Both the performers and the listeners of said music are affected.

Music is a powerful form of communication, whose sole purpose is to evoke a desired response. Music affects listeners in what can be interpreted in both positive and negative ways. Possibly the only separation of the emotional effects of music on the psyche is the controlling emotional barriers/blocks individual Human beings create for their minds. People can become addicted to music and like any addictive substance it can easily contribute to the erosion of common sense. In other words Girls and Boys go insane doing virtually anything for their favorite musical artist even having sex with them and their associates and other things that are fun at the time but can prove to be damaging if left unchecked.

"Why do you think musical artists sing about sex, money, and drugs all the time?"

Musical artist know that impressionable minds will provide the pleasurable amenities that they crave by the truckloads and many of them will be our sweet little sons and daughters. Granted, I am not preaching about not letting kids have fun. Just insist they make smart choices and not stupid ones. Realize what an addiction really is. It is something that produces a pleasurable response and you crave that response and wish to have it satiated as much as possible hopefully without it killing you. Food, drugs, sex, and music feel very good and can definitely fit into the category of addiction.

All human beings relate to sounds that cater to our deep need for acceptance. Music serves as an excitable conduit that provides immediate access to acceptance by the artists we admire and in turn provides the artists with droves of gullible admirers. "Who controls *who* in those backstage situations?"

Case in Point:

Music of a religious nature is incredibly inspirational. Music that is soft and sweet is very calming and can also be seductive. Music that contains inflammatory lyrics and beats can be a time bomb of energy waiting to explode.

Now mix and match:

- Religious music - with inflammatory hate lyrics.
- Seductive music - praising Almighty God.
- Inflammatory lyrics - combined with sexy seductive music.

"Does that work?"

Music is a powerful and influential entertainment stimulus, along with television, video, radio, and movies. I personally love music and I am a firm believer in the freedom of speech so it is up to adults to look out for the welfare of the young people we love. Censorship for adults as an option generally creates problems with freedom of speech but censorship for impressionable kids is advisable.

MUSIC

Wise Elder Tidbit:

If you look at the world of entertainment you will have no problem finding thousands of talented and influential people. Making music is easy even among those who are considered geniuses of their art but to find someone whose actions seek to bring peace and understanding into the world is a rare thing.

> Why is everything that's supposed to be bad / Make me feel so good?
> – *Kanye West - Rapper*

> It's all right letting yourself go as long as you can let yourself back.
> – *Mick Jagger - Rolling Stones*

APPEARANCE

… "How do I look?"… "I'm the CEO of a hot record label"… "So, what's your sign?"

> I caused my husband's heart attack. In the middle of lovemaking I took the paper bag off my head.
> – Joan Rivers

"What is Appearance?"

Appearance is the perceived mental interpretation pictured by the mind of a human being, of itself. Human beings also picture, perceive, judge, and evaluate other human beings, living things, objects, and situations by their "appearances."

Appearance, next to fear and survival, is one of the most powerful driving forces within human beings. Sometimes appearance can cause a more powerful effect than that caused by fear and survival combined. Human beings rarely make a move in society without considering their appearance. Appearance dictates every facet of action or lack of action and people are fascinated with the outer physical appearance of others, themselves, other creatures, and material things. Societies regularly promote or shun people's practices when it comes to modifying the way you look from tummy tucks, breast augmentations, liposuction, tattooing, body modifications (i.e. stretching the neck, branding, scaring, and piercing), and the most drastic of them all, cutting and resetting the bones in the legs to make you taller particularly in China where height is a very powerful status symbol.

Rarely do human beings step outside of their private concerns about personal appearance and oftentimes human beings do not consider inner true appearance as being of any real substantial importance due to endless emotional hang-ups generally rule the existence of appearance for Humans.

APPEARANCE

Case in Point:

"You look like a geek! Find somewhere else to sit!"

"She's the winner of the state beauty pageant!"

"I don't know him personally, but other people say he's gay."

"What kind of car do you drive?"

"Fat people are so lazy!"

"I can't go because I don't have anything suitable to wear."

"I need plastic surgery to continue my career."

"Our country will look weak if we don't attack now."

"I will never get a good job because of the color of my skin."

Statements of this nature affect you and cause reactions synonymous with worrying and self-loathing.

Worrying about appearances causes endless conjecture, storytelling, assuming, and predictions of favorable or bad outcomes suspected by "the talking in your heads." Oftentimes the talking in the head blocks our genius from expression, our experience of self-awareness, and our furthering our very own peace because appearance rides the coat-tails of acceptance, and to humans, remember acceptance = love. It will cause you to act in ways that are detrimental to the oneness that we all are a part of as human beings. If you feel that your appearance makes you better than others, less than others, or separate from others, then you are indeed in a trap of perpetual mental illusion. This will cause you to be easily manipulated by individuals who will pick-up on that energy and use it for what its worth. The reality in which you live is not real; it is a reality created by your programming, not you (the real you makes clear choices because you know you can choose other than listening to the negativity the talking in the head spouts out).

Philosophy of "X": Revealing the True Meaning of Life

> I cried because I had no shoes until I met a man who had no feet.
> *– Persian Saying*

Perfect appearance is an impossible state to achieve. There is no perfect beauty, no matter how much it may seem so and trying for this perfect appearance and piling unfair expectations on top of the premise that there is a perfect appearance, is an astronomical waste of life, resources, and precious time. I'm not saying that if you are attractive to shun and dismiss it or not to have the occasional visit to your plastic surgeon. The body is divine art and we are sexually aroused by what we perceive as beauty so I know you want to look good in that regard. Sex and appearance initiate the reproductive process and it is the initial catalyst for sharing intimacy and that's a healthy normal reaction within a surviving species. Art is meant to be enjoyed, but not to control your life.

Examine your life and see how appearance controls your life by looking at they way you respond to others in social settings. Transform your life by weeding out the illusions your appearance brings and finally begin to experience Peace. You are not your appearance. The outer shell can never even approximate the beauty that makes life grand. Love and understanding of life is beauty, and that beauty is the kind that lasts forever.

Frankly if you think you are all that and better than everybody else, you're not beautiful. You're rat-dog ugly. The conversations that people have about you will be proof of that. So kill that madness right now and let the world love you for you for a change.

> If I were two-faced, would I be wearing this one?
> *– Abraham Lincoln*

> To belittle someone or something to make you look better in the eyes of others is an illusion.
> *–"X"*

IN CONCLUSION

I challenge you to disregard, discredit, and forget the contents of this book. It is completely within your rights to throw it away, burn it, curse it, spit on it, but no matter what you do there is absolutely no refund. Considering that everything in this book was a lie – it may or may not have an impact on you. Just realize that the world needs you, and you are the only you in the world, now and forever.

> I don't know what your destiny will be, but one thing I know: the only ones among you who will be truly happy are those who will have sought and found how to serve.
> – Albert Schweitzer

The way I achieve Peace in my life is to share whatever I have to offer in the way of knowledge, time, and resources with other people, animals, and humanitarian organizations on a daily basis. Giving is the greatest honor I can offer to the experience of God my creator and my fellow human beings. I request that you join me in the game that I play named "PEACEFUL EXPERIENCE." To participate, all you need to do is tackle a problem of such extraordinary magnitude that it keeps you walking towards Peace forever or you can keep playing the game – make all the money you can – and die a greedy anal-retentive shortsighted butt-hole. If that's the game you choose, I'm fine with that, after all God did give you your life and as an enlightened individual I must respect that by the reasoning of the freedom of choice law #321 of the Galactic Code of Inalienable Rights. (I just made that up.)
I will just trust that when you croak (die), a beautiful, loving, peacemaker in the ongoing game of life will recycle your lifetime supply of greed money for the good of all and not for the false hope of self-gratification because you can't take it with you.

So all of you kids standing in line for your inheritance to roll in, start planning on how you will restore dignity and honor to your family name by your generous contributions to the society of your choice. I know that you can, will, and must do what is right to save our deteriorating pollution filled world. If not, I will see you on the other side with the other six billion plus lost souls.

The Tibetan people were once a feared and hated people for their ferocity in warring campaigns throughout Asia. With the influence of one man called the "Dalai Llama", the entire nation dropped their swords and became a peace loving culture, the only time in Human History that an entire nation took such a magnificent stance for the cause of Peace.

> Many persons have the wrong idea of what constitutes true happiness. It is not attained through self-gratification but through fidelity to a worthy cause.
> – Helen Keller

> This giving – I hope it gets to be contagious because it feels so good... I've never been happier than I am today.
> – Ted Turner - After donating $1 billion to worldwide charities.

> In a community in which there is involuntary starvation every well-fed person is a thief.
> – Holbrook Jackson

Peaceful transformation of our world can be done even with the nations of today if the people would take back their God given power. Even our governments are made up of living people (not the big fancy all-inclusive buildings) who can answer to the will of the peacefully protesting masses that they govern. So let's look at a few challenges we can choose to take on in our lives. Pick one or more and act today:

"X-ISM'S" PROBLEMS WORTH LIVING FOR

Save endangered species and enforce humane treatment of livestock and pets.

Provide food, shelter, and job education for the homeless.

Sponsor job employment and job/trade/emotional management education to rehabilitate ex-convicts giving much needed second chances.

End teenage violence in the African – American community by creating educational programs that specifically address this issue.

Provide free and discounted healthcare to people who can't afford it in western countries were health care makes trillions but gives back little or nothing to struggling decent citizens.

Construct scholarship programs to educate and enlighten poor people to create a more peaceful uniformity between the social classes.

Make an organized peaceful stand against unjust wars.

Peacefully force the governments and corporations of industrialized nations to clean up the environment and provide affordable cleaner alternatives for energy production and transportation.

Create free or affordable clinics that will treat obesity as an addiction disease and help people rebuild their lives.

Demand that huge fast-food chains carry healthy vegetarian selections that are tasty and affordable. So people can help themselves maintain their health (Burger King fast-food restaurants offers Vegetarian Burgers).

Provide intervention and recovery programs for drug addicts.

Save the rain forest from total destruction by greedy land developers.

Create exciting vocational and art programs for poor children, orphaned or neglected.

Adopt a child to give them a chance for a decent life.

Educate children and teenagers on sex, to prevent unwanted pregnancies, sexually transmitted diseases, and sexual molestations and supply whatever goods necessary to keep youths safe. Parents really need to ban together in more public forums to scientifically address these issues so that they will be comfortable with what information they will allow schools/churches/ institutions to teach their children about sex.

Stop being apathetic and participate in the governmental elective process. Once the people are elected into public office complaining about the way they run your world is probably – to little to late.

Peacefully force the governments and major world corporations to provide fair wages to employees worldwide.

Make a stand against racism, and inequality in the justice and corporate systems.

Aid victims of domestic violence by providing protection, food, therapy, and safe shelter with security systems in place so they can get a fresh start in life.

Peacefully demand that China frees Tibet so that the Dalai Lama can return home to teach and love his people in peace.

China needs to enforce environmental laws and clean up its polluted lands, which are giving cancer to millions of poor defenseless citizens so that greedy corporate executives can stuff their coffers with ill-gotten gains.

Demand that America update its lagging educational system that is nowhere near the top percentile in worldwide educational polls.

IN CONCLUSION

Support businesses and corporations (i.e. car companies, utility companies, new fuel alternative companies), which will create and distribute better non-polluting means of fueling the country and demand that the government support and fund programs that will ultimately save our planet.

These are just some things you may want to consider to enrich your life. Being that there is only six degrees of separation on earth for all Human beings there is no doubt that one or more of these problems will be paying you a visit soon (if they haven't visited you already, or visiting you right now). So pay them a visit first.

So my friends:

Be aware of the power of creation that you possess.

Be aware that you, and only you, call the shots in your life. You invent your life every day. Invent a happy life you cannot even imagine being possible and that is only the starting point of what you are.

Be aware that you are a computer of the grandest design ever conceived. You have the power to negotiate the terms of your lifetime of programming. Visualize, be joyful and grateful, and what you want out of life your mind/computer will make a way to manifest it for you.

Be aware that *"the talking in the head"* can and must be acknowledged, and then disregarded it if the mental chatter disrupts your quest for peace. It does not wish you to be at peace – ever, for its own survival's sake. Disarm it! Know that *"the talking in the head"* is not you and that your greatness is beyond measure.

Be aware that you are at one with all things and with life.

Be aware that you never truly die.

Be aware that the author of this book accepts and loves you just the way that you are — imperfect, alive, and complete.

> Everyone is crazy; some just show it more than others.
> – "X"

Divine Peace and Blessings,
– "X"